Recipes for
FAT FREE LIVING
COOKBOOK

EVERY RECIPE
UNDER 1 GRAM OF FAT
PER SERVING

Recipes for FAT FREE LIVING COOKBOOK 1

ISBN 0-9636876-6-2
Jyl Steinback
Fat Free Living, Inc.
15202 North 50th Place
Scottsdale, Arizona   85254
602-996-6300

This book made it to your book shelves thanks to the time and energy of many people.

First thank you, to all the aerobic, fitness, and fat-free eaters for your positive encouragement and recipe suggestions. You all outdid yourselves and helped make this book possible!

Thank you to my outstanding mom and dad, Betty and Bill Levy (one of my favorite fat-free eaters), who always give of themselves to make all of my dreams come true. (And there have been a lot of dreams)! You're the greatest and I love you very much!

Thanks Jacie, one of my other very favorite fat-free eaters and sister, for all your love and support, and for helping me with so many recipes and all of the editing. I love you.

Thanks Jeff, (my brother), and Diane (my sister-in-law), another of my very favorite fat-free eaters. I appreciate all your love, support, and wonderful ideas. You're always coming through when I'm in a crunch! I love you both lots.

Thanks Alex for just being here!

Thanks Snooky and Harlan (my mother and father-in-law) for being my very best sales people ever. Thanks for believing in me and helping *Fat Free Living* become a huge success. I love you both very much!

Thanks Karen for a wonderful idea for a fabulous book. You're a great friend and I appreciate and love you lots!

Thanks Jamie for being the best daughter a mom can ask for. I love you very much! I appreciated the use of your favorite chair and sorry I was always on the phone. You're the greatest in the world! Lucky ME!

And Gary, my other half, and my very favorite person in the world. You're THE BEST! You're patient, a great listener, a wonderful friend, and thanks for believing in me! I love you more than life!

PREFACE

What I'm trying to give you in this book is an assortment of recipes that will help you prepare meals with the barest hint of fat. We think that it's just impossible to truly eliminate all of the fat grams from your diet. But, believe me, these recipes are about as low as you can go. These recipes have been gathered from numerous "aerobic, fitness trainers, and fat-free eaters" throughout the United States who are happy to share with you the food preparations which they enjoy.

When you visit your supermarket, read the labels on the food items. What you want is a label that says, "Fat......0 grams." New fat free items are appearing in the supermarkets almost on a daily basis. Just look for them!

My experience shows that you will not notice much of a change for about three weeks. However, after that, if you have been a faithful "FAT FREE FOLLOWER", you will suddenly find that pounds are disappearing, as well as inches. You will be on your way. Remember, good eating always is enhanced with exercise. If you combine the two, the end result will be yours that much sooner.

So, have fun and enjoy the "new" you.

Do you have a picture in your mind of how you would like your body to look? I believe that your body can actually begin to resemble your "mind picture" through a simplified eating plan.

"Fat Free Living" is the newest, healthiest and most sensible method of eating today! If you stick with fat free foods, you can pretty well eat whatever and whenever you want and still not be hungry. Sounds great to me! During the 1980s, the password was "think thin" (and not surprisingly, most of us did just that, thought about it). But now the byword for the 90s is "live slim", and if we learned anything during the last decade, it's that the vast majority of the "overweighters" will never become thin by reducing their intake. The old joke, that over the past ten years my brother-in-law has lost eleven hundred and fifty pounds and gained twelve hundred and twenty five pounds, is really not a laughing matter, and probably a good mirror for almost every overweight person you know. The extra pounds not only affect your appearance, but are detrimental to good health. For years the Surgeon General has been talking about high blood cholesterol as a major risk factor for coronary heart disease and specifically that the amount and types of fat in the diet adversely affect blood cholesterol.

Today, however, there is a genuinely effective weapon to assist in weight reduction, and that's eating LESS FAT! Eating foods without fat not only helps you reduce your poundage in a slow and sensible manner, but also helps you shed inches. Best of all, with a carefully planned set of exercises, your inches will disappear from all over your body. "FAT FREE LIVING" is the road to follow to reach the new you.

"FAT FREE LIVING" is a way of life! Eating less fat is the way to make you feel better and healthier mentally and physically. Once you incorporate "FAT FREE LIVING" into your life your self esteem and "body image" will improve a hundred fold. You will like you and have lots of energy to enjoy the new, healthier you!

FAT FREE FABULOUS FOODS

Appealing Appetizers

Super Salads

Exciting Eggs

Vigorous Vegetables

Scrumptious Side Dishes

Bravo Breads

Magnificent Main Courses

Sensational Snacks

Spectacular Soups

Delectable Desserts

Desirable Drinks

Magnificent Menu

Fabulous Fat Counter

APPEALING APPETIZERS

FAT FREE CHIPS

ingredients: 12 7" corn tortillas

directions: Cut tortillas into fourths.
Spray cookie sheet with Pam.
Place cut-up tortillas on a cookie sheet.
Broil for a couple of minutes and flip them over and broil the other side for a couple of minutes.

Delicious and crunchy!

Serves: 12

Nutrition per serving

Calories	56
Protein	1 g.
Carbohydrate	12 g.
Cholesterol	0 mg.
Sodium	40 mg.
Dietary Fiber	1.3 g.

Exchanges
3/4 bread

Cindy Muhleman, Scottsdale, Arizona

NACHOS

ingredients: 48 fat free chips
2 cups favorite kind of fat free cheese

directions: Spread the fat free chips over a plate.
Sprinkle the fat free cheese over the top
of every chip.
Put in the microwave for 1 to 2 minutes, or
until the cheese is totally melted.

What a wonderful appetizer or snack.
GREAT CRUNCH!

Serves: 6

Nutrition per serving

Calories	83
Protein	3 g.
Carbohydrate	15 g.
Cholesterol	2 mg.
Sodium	67 mg.
Dietary Fiber	1.2 g.

Exchanges
1/2 starch
1 meat

SALSA DIP

ingredients: 1 cup salsa
1 cup non fat plain yogurt

directions: Mix well and refrigerate.

Serves: 4

Nutrition per serving

Calories	52
Protein	3 g.
Carbohydrate	8 g.
Cholesterol	1 mg.
Sodium	683 mg.
Dietary Fiber	0 g.

Exchanges

1/2 milk
1/2 vegetable

Jill Reinke, Scottsdale, Arizona

DIJON DIP

ingredients: 2 cups non fat yogurt
2 cups fat free Dijon mustard
1/2 cup snipped fresh chives
1 T. fresh lemon juice

directions: Combine yogurt, mustard and chives in a bowl.
Whisk until blended.
Chill.
Add fresh lemon juice to taste when used.

Serves: 8

Nutrition per serving		**Exchanges**
Calories	129	1 1/2 milk
Protein	3 g.	
Carbohydrate	5 g.	
Cholesterol	1 mg.	
Sodium	1604 mg.	
Dietary Fiber	.1 g.	

Chuck Browning, Phoenix, Arizona. My career as a fitness professional includes my B.S. in Physiology/ Kinesiology, A.C.E. certification in Aerobics for 5 years, A.C.E. certification in Personal Training for 3 years, and 11 years experience in teaching aerobics and personal training.

ONION DIP

ingredients: 1 cup non fat plain yogurt
1/2 T. chopped onion, dried

directions: Mix well and refrigerate.

Serves: 4

Nutrition per serving

Calories	32
Protein	3 g.
Carbohydrate	4 g.
Cholesterol	1 mg.
Sodium	48 mg.
Dietary Fiber	0 g.

Exchanges
1/2 milk

Jill Reinke, Scottsdale, Arizona

COTTAGE CHEESE DIP

ingredients: 2 pounds (32 oz.) non fat cottage cheese
1/2 medium onion, diced
1/2 green bell pepper, diced
1 large carrot (or 2 small), diced
dash of pepper and "No Salt" to taste

directions: Mix above ingredients.
Season to taste.
Return to refrigerator and chill at least 2 hours.
Serve with vegetables, no fat pretzels, or your
favorite chips and crackers (no fat of course).

Serves: 8

Nutrition per serving
Calories	28
Protein	4 g.
Carbohydrate	3 g.
Cholesterol	0 mg.
Sodium	96 mg.
Dietary Fiber	.5 g.

Exchanges
1/2 meat

Jill Reinke, Scottsdale, Arizona

GREEN CHILI

ingredients: 2 cups fresh or frozen green chili, chopped
1 medium onion, chopped
1 clove garlic, minced

Combine above in sauce pan with:
2 cups water
1 T. oregano
1 t. ground cumin
1 t. salt

directions: Cover and cook gently until onion is soft.
Serve over beans and rice or posole.

Note: Can be thickened with 1 T. cornstarch.

Serves: 4

Nutrition per serving		**Exchanges**
Calories	43	2 vegetable
Protein	2 g.	
Carbohydrate	10 g.	
Cholesterol	0 mg.	
Sodium	680 mg.	
Dietary Fiber	1.9 g.	

JoAnn Bishop, New Mexico Representative: IDEA

KIWI
PINEAPPLE SALSA

ingredients: 4 small kiwi fruit, peeled and diced
1/2 cup diced pineapple
1/4 red or green bell pepper, diced
2 T. diced red onion
1/4 cup minced chives
2 cups vegetable stock
1 t. ground black pepper
2 T. chopped scallions
1 mango diced

directions: In medium mixing bowl, combine ingredients and toss together.
Cover bowl and refrigerate until chilled.

Serve kiwi pineapple salsa over fish.

Serves: 4

Nutrition per serving		Exchanges
Calories	110	2 fruit
Protein	3 g.	
Carbohydrate	26 g.	
Cholesterol	0 mg.	
Sodium	241 mg.	
Dietary Fiber	4.5 g.	

SPINACH DIP

ingredients: 1 package frozen chopped spinach,
cooked and drained
1 cup fat free mayo
1/2 cup scallions, chopped
1 package Knorr veggie soup mix
1/2 cup basil, chopped

directions: Cook and drain spinach.
Mix all other ingredients together and then blend
with spinach.
Cover and refrigerate for a few hours.
Best served at room temperature.

Serves: 4

Nutrition per serving

Calories	100
Protein	4 g.
Carbohydrate	23 g.
Cholesterol	0 mg.
Sodium	1028 mg.
Dietary Fiber	4.1 g.

Exchanges

1 vegetable
1 starch

*Karen Carnow, Phoenix, Arizona. I am an aerobic
instructor at U.S. Swim and Fitness and a personal
trainer in people's homes. I love staying in shape
and helping others do the same.*

HAWAIIAN PUPU

ingredients: 1 pound cooked shrimp
1/2 head of green cabbage
2 limes
1/4 cup cocktail sauce

directions: Shred cabbage on platter.
Spread shrimp on cabbage.
Squeeze lime juice on shrimp.
Use sauce as a dip.

Enjoy this delicious low-cal appetizer.

Serves: 8

Nutrition per serving		Exchanges
Calories	86	1 1/2 meat
Protein	13 g.	
Carbohydrate	7 g.	
Cholesterol	111 mg.	
Sodium	268 mg.	
Dietary Fiber	.6 g.	

Rebecca Lunden-Draeger, RLD Body Works, Kailua, Hawaii

FAT FREE
YOGURT DIP

ingredients: 1 10 oz. container of plain nonfat yogurt
1 package Good Seasons Fat Free Italian Dressing

directions: Mix the two above ingredients and serve
with a wonderful vegetable plate.

Simple and outstanding! Your company
will love it and so will you!

Serves: 3

Nutrition per serving

Calories	54
Protein	5 g.
Carbohydrate	8 g.
Cholesterol	2 mg.
Sodium	179 mg.
Dietary Fiber	0 g.

Exchanges
1/2 milk

CRUDITE DIP

ingredients:　1/4 cup prepared mustard
1/3 cup plain nonfat yogurt
1/4 cup fat free mayo
1 T. chopped chives
1/4 T. garlic powder
1 T. chopped basil

directions:　Blend and chill.
Serve with raw veggies.

Serves: 4

Nutrition per serving		Exchanges
Calories	37	1/2 starch
Protein	2 g.	
Carbohydrate	6 g.	
Cholesterol	0 mg.	
Sodium	393 mg.	
Dietary Fiber	.6 g.	

Karen Carnow, Phoenix, Arizona

CELERY STUFFED WITH HERBED NON FAT CHEESE

ingredients: 16 tender celery stalks, leaves on
1 cup non fat cream cheese, blended with
4 T. skim milk
1 T. chopped fresh coriander (cilantro)
1 T. chopped fresh basil
1 T. chopped fresh chives
1 garlic clove, put through a garlic press
pinch of Tang
add Spike and pepper to taste

directions:

Wash and dry the celery stalks.
In a small bowl, mix together all the remaining ingredients.
Spread the filling in the stalks with a small knife or spatula.

May add scallions for variety.

Crisp celery stalks are filled with a creamy blend of cream cheese, Tang, coriander, fresh basil and chives.

Serves: 8

Nutrition per serving

Calories	48
Protein	6 g.
Carbohydrate	6 g.
Cholesterol	5 mg.
Sodium	234 mg.
Dietary Fiber	1.5 g.

Exchanges
1 vegetable
1/2 meat

SKINNY DIP

ingredients: 1/2 cup plain non fat yogurt
1/4 t. dill weed
1 t. minced onion
1/8 t. salt
1/2 packet Equal brand sweetener

directions: Mix all ingredients thoroughly.
Chill several hours.
Serve with crisp raw vegetables.

Serves: 2

Nutrition per serving

Calories	33
Protein	3 g.
Carbohydrate	5 g.
Cholesterol	1 mg.
Sodium	183 mg.
Dietary Fiber	0 g.

Exchanges
1/3 milk

Kathy Schievelbein, Bloomington, Minnesota

FAT FREE
POTATO SKINS

ingredients: 1 large potato
2 slices fat free cheese
2 T. fat free sour cream

directions: Cook potato in microwave for 8 to 10 minutes.
Slice potato in 4 sections.
Scoop out the insides.
Take 1/2 piece of cheese and lay it over each
1/4 of potato.
Put in toaster oven and toast as if it was a
slice of bread.
The cheese should melt over the 4 slices of potato.
Get your fat free sour cream and start dipping!

These potato skins are simple and sensational!

Serves: 1

Nutrition per serving

Calories	168
Protein	14 g.
Carbohydrate	29 g.
Cholesterol	10 mg.
Sodium	647 mg.
Dietary Fiber	1.8 g.

Exchanges

1 starch
1 1/2 meat

COWBOY CAVIAR

ingredients:
8 oz. dried black-eyed peas
1 red pepper, diced
2 green scallions, diced
2 bottles jalapeno peppers in vinegar
(or nacho flavored), drained and minced
2 T. lemon juice
1 T. dijon mustard
2 cloves garlic
1 t. salt
1 t. thyme leaves
1 t. sugar
1/4 t. tabasco
pepper to taste
1/4 cup non fat dressing (Italian)

directions:
Soak beans overnight.
Put in pot - boil, simmer 35-40 minutes.
Drain and rinse in cold water.
Put into big bowl and add all the other
above ingredients.
Toss and mix.
Serve at room temperature.

Serves: 6

Nutrition per serving		Exchanges
Calories	59	2 vegetable
Protein	2 g.	
Carbohydrate	14 g.	
Cholesterol	1 mg.	
Sodium	1386 mg.	
Dietary Fiber	1.4 g.	

Cheryl Hewett, Aerobics teacher for Bally's
U.S. Swim and Fitness, Phoenix, Arizona

CRAB SALAD SPREAD

ingredients: 1/3 cup non fat mayonnaise
3 T. minced onion
1 t. lemon juice
dash of salt (optional)
dash of pepper
8 oz. fat free crab
1/2 cup chopped celery

directions: In a medium size bowl, mix mayonnaise,
lemon juice, salt and pepper until blended.
Stir in crab or shrimp and celery.

Can be used to stuff tomatoes, artichokes or
hard boiled egg whites.

Can also be used for spread on sandwiches.

Serves: 2

Nutrition per serving		Exchanges
Calories	147	2 meat
Protein	12 g.	2 vegetable
Carbohydrate	23 g.	
Cholesterol	13 mg.	
Sodium	722 mg.	
Dietary Fiber	.7 g.	

SOUTHWEST SALSA

ingredients: 3/4 cup diced husked tomatillos* (about 8 medium)
1/4 cup diced red bell pepper
1/4 cup diced red onion
3 T. tarragon
2 T. orange juice
2 T. fresh lime juice
1 T. sugar
1/2 t. minced seeded jalapeno chili

directions: Puree 1/4 cup tomatillos in processor.
Pour into medium bowl.
Mix in remaining tomatillos and all ingredients.
Cover and refrigerate at least 30 minutes.

Can be prepared 1 day ahead.

*A tomatillo resembles a green tomato with a
paper-thin husk.

Serves: 4

Nutrition per serving		**Exchanges**
Calories	42	2 vegetable
Protein	1 g.	
Carbohydrate	9 g.	
Cholesterol	0 mg.	
Sodium	8 mg.	
Dietary Fiber	1.1 g.	

PITA CHIPS

ingredients: 1 round non fat pita bread (pocket)

directions: Preheat oven to 350°
Split pita into two rounds.
Cut each in to 8 wedges.
Place in a single layer on cookie sheet.
Bake 8 to 10 minutes, until crisp.
Spray lightly with Pam and sprinkle
with garlic powder.
Cool and store in closed container.

Serves: 2

Nutrition per serving

Calories	82
Protein	2.7 g.
Carbohydrate	17 g.
Cholesterol	0 mg.
Sodium	161 mg.
Dietary Fiber	.5 g.

Exchanges
1 bread

CURRY DIP

ingredients: 1 cup fat free mayonnaise
1 t. worcestershire
1 t. garlic powder
1 t. curry powder
1 t. tarragon vinegar
1 t. white horseradish

directions: Mix all ingredients.
Cover and refrigerate.

Serves: 4

Nutrition per serving

Calories	54
Protein	.2 g.
Carbohydrate	13 g.
Cholesterol	0 mg.
Sodium	776 mg.
Dietary Fiber	.2 g.

Exchanges
1/2 starch

SPINACH STUFFED MUSHROOMS

ingredients: 1 pound mushrooms
1 package frozen spinach - cook and drain
1/2 cup non fat plain yogurt
1/2 cup non fat mayonnaise
1/4 cup chopped onions
1 cup non fat cheese (Alpine Lace cheddar or mozzarella)
Butter Buds, salt, pepper and Spike

directions: Clean mushrooms and remove stems.
Chop mushrooms.
Brown mushrooms using Pam in a Teflon pan.
Cook and drain spinach.
Whip with non fat plain yogurt and mayonnaise.
Saute finely chopped onions and stems.
Mix with spinach.
Stuff in caps.
Sprinkle with non fat cheese, Butter Buds, salt, pepper, and Spike.

Serves: 4

Nutrition per serving		Exchanges
Calories	98	2 vegetable
Protein	8 g.	1 meat
Cholesterol	2 mg.	
Sodium	546 mg.	
Dietary Fiber	3.6 g.	

Karen Carnow: Phoenix, Arizona

21

SUPER
SALADS

CAESAR SALAD

ingredients: 1 head romaine lettuce
1/2 cup fat free ranch dressing
1/2 cup fat free peppercorn dressing
1 cup fat free croutons
ground pepper to taste

directions: Cut romaine lettuce into bite size pieces.
Mix with ranch and peppercorn dressings,
fat free croutons and pepper.

Serves: 4

Nutrition per serving

Calories	108
Protein	3 g.
Carbohydrate	19 g.
Cholesterol	0 mg.
Sodium	627 mg.
Dietary Fiber	3.4 g.

Exchanges

3 vegetable
1/2 bread

Betty and Bill Levy, St. Louis, Missouri

FAT FREE CROUTONS

ingredients: 1 loaf sourdough bread (12 slices)
6 T. Butter Buds

directions: Cut bread into 1 inch slices.
Sprinkle with Butter Buds, covering completely.
Let stand 2 minutes.
Turn and sprinkle other side.
Cut into crouton size pieces.
Put into brownie tin and cook at 350°
(about 20 minutes) or until golden in color.

Absolutely the very best for salads, soups
and just munching!

Serves: 8

Nutrition per serving		Exchanges
Calories	74	1 starch
Protein	3 g.	
Carbohydrate	14 g.	
Cholesterol	3 mg.	
Sodium	349 mg.	
Dietary Fiber	3.8 g.	

Betty and Bill Levy, St. Louis, Missouri

MARINATED SALAD

ingredients: 1/2 cup fat free Italian dressing
                   pepper to taste
                   1 large cucumber, sliced thin
                   1 small onion, sliced thin
                   5 radishes, sliced thin

directions: Combine first 2 ingredients in bowl.
                   Add vegetables.
                   Toss.
                   Cover and refrigerate.

                   Serves: 2

Nutrition per serving
Calories	60
Protein	2 g.
Carbohydrate	24 g.
Cholesterol	0 mg.
Sodium	1120 mg.
Dietary Fiber	2.3 g.

Exchanges
2 vegetable

MINTED
CUCUMBER SALAD

ingredients: 1 cup fresh mint leaves, chopped fine
1/2 cup non fat Italian dressing
1/4 cup red wine vinegar
2 cucumbers, peeled and sliced

directions: Mix mint leaves, dressing and vinegar.
Chill.
Toss over cucumbers.

Serves: 4

Nutrition per serving		Exchanges
Calories	59	2 vegetable
Protein	3 g.	
Carbohydrate	16 g.	
Cholesterol	0 mg.	
Sodium	432 mg.	
Dietary Fiber	1.2 g.	

Karen Carnow, Phoenix, Arizona

TOMATO SALAD

ingredients: 1 large tomato, sliced
1 medium sweet onion, sliced
1 cucumber, thinly sliced
fresh basil leaf
salt and pepper to taste
1 cup Italian fat free salad dressing

directions: Alternately place tomato slices, onion slices, cucumber slices and fresh basil leaf in a bowl. Pour on salad dressing. Add salt and pepper to taste. Remove basil leaf before serving.

Serves: 4

Nutrition per serving

Calories	64
Protein	1 g.
Carbohydrate	36 g.
Cholesterol	0 mg.
Sodium	1684 mg.
Dietary Fiber	.9 g.

Exchanges

2 vegetable
1/4 starch

COLE SLAW

ingredients: 1 cup cabbage, shredded
1/2 cup carrots, shredded
1/4 cup onion, chopped
1 t. parsley, minced
1/2 cup chopped sweet red pepper, optional
1/4 cup vinegar
1/4 cup fat free Italian dressing
1/8 t. pepper
1 T. Sweet 'N Low

directions: Combine first 5 ingredients in a large bowl.
Mix Italian dressing, vinegar, Sweet 'N Low and
pepper.
Shake.
Pour mixture over vegetables and mix together.
Refrigerate and cover.

Serves: 4

Nutrition per serving

Calories	37
Protein	1 g.
Carbohydrate	12 g.
Cholesterol	0 mg.
Sodium	269 mg.
Dietary Fiber	1.3 g.

Exchanges
1 1/2 vegetable

WALDORF SALAD

ingredients: 3 apples, diced
1 T. juice of lemon
1/4 cup raisins
1 cup celery, diced
3/4 cup fat free vanilla yogurt

directions: Sprinkle lemon juice over apples to prevent discoloring.
Toss with yogurt and refrigerate.

Serves: 4

Nutrition per serving

Calories	133	
Protein	2.9 g.	
Carbohydrate	32 g.	
Cholesterol	1 mg.	
Sodium	57 mg.	
Dietary Fiber	3.7 g.	

Exchanges
3/4 milk
1 fruit

CARROT SALAD

ingredients:
1/2 cup golden raisins
1/4 cup cider vinegar
2 pounds carrots, peeled and grated
3/4 cup non fat Italian dressing
1 T. sugar
salt and pepper
dash of cinnamon or nutmeg
finely chopped parsley

directions:
Soak the raisins in the vinegar for 30 minutes.
Drain, reserve the vinegar.
Mix raisins with the carrots.
Add the vinegar to the non fat Italian dressing.
Season with salt and pepper.
Add cinnamon or nutmeg for additional flavor.
Mix with carrots and raisins.
Sprinkle with parsley.

Serves: 4

Nutrition per serving		Exchanges
Calories	185	5 vegetable
Protein	3 g.	1 fruit
Carbohydrate	53 g.	
Cholesterol	0 mg.	
Sodium	712 mg.	
Dietary Fiber	7.5 g.	

CRANBERRY-ORANGE CHEESE MOLD

ingredients:
1 1/2 cups boiling water
1 large package cranberry flavored Jell-O gelatin
1 1/2 cups cold water
1/2 t. cinnamon
1 navel orange, peeled and chopped
1 cup whole berry cranberry sauce
8 oz. fat free cream cheese, softened

directions:
Place gelatin into large bowl. Pour in boiling water and stir until gelatin is completely dissolved.
Stir in cold water and cinnamon.
Reserve 1 cup gelatin and pour remaining 2 cups of gelatin into medium bowl.
Refrigerate 1-2 hours or until thickened.
Stir chopped orange and cranberry sauce into thickened gelatin and place in a 6-cup mold or 9" x 13" baking dish.
Refrigerate 30 minutes or until set.
Stir reserved 1 cup of gelatin into cream cheese and mix until smooth.
Pour over gelatin layer and refrigerate 4 hours or until firm.

Serves: 12

Nutrition per serving

Calories	59
Protein	12 g.
Carbohydrate	3 g.
Cholesterol	3 mg.
Sodium	18 mg.
Dietary Fiber	.3 g.

Exchanges
1 fruit

31

SPINACH SALAD WITH MANDARIN DRESSING

ingredients: 4 cups fresh spinach leaves
2 cups cherry tomatoes
1 cup thinly sliced radishes
1/2 cup non fat croutons
1/2 cup mushrooms

dressing:
1/4 cup non fat Italian dressing
2 T. low sodium soy sauce
1 t. vinegar
2 T. sugar
1/8 t. pepper

directions: Combine all dressing ingredients in a jar.
Cover tightly.
Refrigerate 2 or more hours.

Wash spinach leaves in cold water and drain.
Remove stems and discard.
Place spinach in large bowl.
Add tomatoes, radishes, mushrooms and croutons.
Add dressing and toss.

Serves: 4

Nutrition per serving		Exchanges
Calories	83	3 1/2 vegetable
Protein	3 g.	
Carbohydrate	20 g.	
Cholesterol	0 mg.	
Sodium	473 mg.	
Dietary Fiber	3.2 g.	

PARTY SCALLOPS

ingredients: 2 cups cooked scallops
2 cups celery, diced
6 hard cooked egg whites, diced
1/2 cup fat free mayonnaise
2 cups seedless green grapes cut in halves

directions: Mix all together and chill.

Serves: 6

Nutrition per serving
Calories	141
Protein	18 g.
Carbohydrate	16 g.
Cholesterol	26 mg.
Sodium	475 mg.
Dietary Fiber	1.5 g.

Exchanges
3 meat
1 fruit

Amy Leroy, Mrs. Arizona-America 1991. She is the fitness director at the Princess Hotel in Scottsdale, Arizona. She also directs the Arizona Angels. Amy is a trainer for the American Aerobic Association International, Princeton University, and also is IDEA and ACE certified.

TRI-COLOR NOODLE SALAD

ingredients: 1 6 oz. package of tri-color noodles
1 6 oz. package of small elbow macaroni or any other small shape pasta
6 hard boiled eggs, chopped (discard yolks)
4 stalks celery, finely chopped
1/2 onion, chopped
1/2 red pepper, chopped
1/2 green pepper, chopped
1 carrot, shredded
1 cup fat free mayonnaise
1/2 cup fat free ranch dressing
1/2 cup plain non fat yogurt

directions: Cook first two ingredients according to package directions.
Combine all ingredients.
Salt and pepper, garlic powder and onion powder to taste.
Sprinkle top with paprika.

Serves: 8

Nutrition per serving
Calories	230
Protein	9 g.
Carbohydrate	45 g.
Cholesterol	0 mg.
Sodium	640 mg.
Dietary Fiber	2 g.

Exchanges
2 starch
1 meat
1 vegetable

CARROT-RAISIN SALAD

ingredients: 2 cups grated carrots
1/2 cup raisins
1/4 cup plain non fat yogurt
1/4 cup non fat mayonnaise
1 t. sugar

directions: Combine all ingredients in mixing bowl.
Toss to blend.
Chill 1 hour or more before serving.

Serves: 2

Nutrition per serving

Calories	204
Protein	4 g.
Carbohydrate	50 g.
Cholesterol	1 mg.
Sodium	445 mg.
Dietary Fiber	4.8 g.

Exchanges

2 fruit
2 vegetable
1/2 starch

SQUASH SALAD

ingredients: 2 medium yellow squash, thinly sliced
2 medium zucchini, thinly sliced
3 cups cooked fat free rice
1/4 red onion, thinly sliced

dressing:
1/2 cup red wine vinegar
1/2 cup fat free Italian dressing
(mix the two above)
1 T. chopped parsley
1 T. chopped dill
salt and pepper to taste

directions: Shake dressing ingredients.
Mix vegetables and rice.
Combine all above and chill to serve.

Serves: 4

Nutrition per serving		Exchanges
Calories	197	1 1/2 vegetable
Protein	5 g.	2 starch
Carbohydrate	51 g.	
Cholesterol	0 mg.	
Sodium	430 mg.	
Dietary Fiber	2.3 g.	

JICAMA AND ORANGE SALAD

ingredients: 1 large jicama, peeled, sliced paper thin
3 oranges, peeled, sectioned
1 red onion, thinly sliced
6 T. lime juice
1/2 cup non fat Italian dressing
6 T. red wine vinegar
1 T. fresh parsley, chopped fine
2 T. fresh cilantro, chopped fine

directions: Line plate with romaine lettuce leaves.
Arrange jicama and oranges in a colorful pattern.
Shake other ingredients.
Pour and chill.

Serves: 4

Nutrition per serving

Calories	92
Protein	3 g.
Carbohydrate	34 g.
Cholesterol	0 mg.
Sodium	431 mg.
Dietary Fiber	5.1 g.

Exchanges

1 fruit
1 vegetable

Karen Carnow, Phoenix, Arizona

TACO SALAD

ingredients:
1 cup shredded lettuce
1 cup chopped tomatoes
1/2 cup chopped scallions
2 cups drained kidney beans
1 cup drained black beans
1 cup grated non fat cheese
3 corn tortillas
1 cup salsa

directions:
Cut corn tortillas into 6 wedges.
Bake at 350° for 7 minutes.
Place cooked corn tortillas on plate.
Place above ingredients on top.
Dollop with one cup salsa.
Drizzle with non fat Italian dressing.

Serves: 5

Nutrition per serving		Exchanges
Calories	154	1 starch
Protein	9 g.	1/2 meat
Carbohydrate	29 g.	2 vegetable
Cholesterol	1 mg.	
Sodium	937 mg.	
Dietary Fiber	1.6 g.	

Karen Carnow, Phoenix, Arizona

JYL'S FAT FREE CAESAR SALAD

ingredients: 2 heads of romaine lettuce
1 1/2 cups Weight Watcher's nonfat grated Parmesan cheese
2 cups fat free homemade croutons (see recipe p. 24)
1 cup Marzetti fat free ranch dressing

directions: Cut and clean 2 heads of romaine lettuce.
Sprinkle nonfat grated Parmesan cheese onto the lettuce.
Add ranch dressing and mix together.
Add more Parmesan cheese and more dressing if needed.
Mix in croutons.

Enjoy!

Serves: 6

Nutrition per serving

Calories	161
Protein	12 g.
Carbohydrate	26 g.
Cholesterol	21 mg.
Sodium	616 mg.
Dietary Fiber	4.6 g.

Exchanges

1 vegetable
1 1/2 starch

VEGETABLE
PITA SALAD

ingredients: 1/2 cup orange segments
1/2 cup finely diced celery
1 cup finely diced fennel
2 T. chopped parsley
1/4 cup chopped onion
2 T. finely chopped cilantro
1 cup Dijon dip (see recipe)
sandwich whole wheat pita pockets, halved
2 tomatoes, thinly sliced
1 cup alfalfa sprouts
1 cup fat free Dijon mustard

directions: Combine all the ingredients for the salad in
a bowl and chill.
In pita half, place 2 tomato slices, some sprouts,
one leaf of spinach and 1/2 cup salad.

Serves: 4

Nutrition per serving   **Exchanges**
Calories   287   2 vegetable
Protein   7 g.   3 starch
Carbohydrate   29 g.
Cholesterol   1 mg.
Sodium   2601 mg.
Dietary Fiber   2.6 g.

Chuck Browing, Phoenix, Arizona

TOMATO
ONION SALAD

ingredients: 2 tomatoes
                   1 sweet onion

directions: Slice tomatoes.
                   Put sweet onion in ice water for 15 minutes.
                   Slice onion.
                   Alternate slices of tomato and onion.
                   Top with your favorite fat free dressing.

                   Serves: 2

Nutrition per serving   **Exchanges**
(without dressing)
Calories   40   1 1/2 vegetable
Protein   2 g.
Carbohydrate   9 g.
Cholesterol   0 mg.
Sodium   286 mg.
Dietary Fiber   2.3 g.

Betty and Bill Levy, St. Louis, Missouri

SANTA FE
CRAB SALAD

ingredients: dressing:
4 small scallions, chopped
1 cup chopped fresh cilantro
1 cup fresh lime juice
2 T. fat free Italian dressing
1 jalapeno chili, halved
1 t. salt
1 T. sugar

salad:
1 1/2 cup corn kernels (fresh or frozen)
1 15 oz. can black beans, rinsed and drained
1 medium zucchini, diced
1 large red bell pepper, diced
3/4 cup diced red onion
1 1/4 pounds fat free crab

directions: Blend first 7 ingredients in blender or food processor until smooth as possible.
(Dressing can be prepared 1 day ahead).
Combine corn, beans, zucchini, bell pepper and red onion in large bowl.
Cut shrimp into pieces and add to vegetables.
Toss with enough dressing to season to taste.
Cover and refrigerate at least 1 hour, up to 6 hours.

Serves: 6

Nutrition per serving		Exchanges
Calories	237	1 meat
Protein	17 g.	1 vegetable
Carbohydrate	44 g.	2 starch
Cholesterol	11 mg.	
Sodium	843 mg.	
Dietary Fiber	5.8 g.	

Valerie Jiuditta, Phoenix, Arizona.
Personal Trainer at U.S. Swim and Fitness.

RED JELL-O SALAD

ingredients: 1 large package cherry or strawberry sugar free Jell-o
(use powdered form of Jell-o)
8 oz. non fat cottage cheese
8 oz. fat free Cool Whip
1 cup fruit cocktail, drained

directions: Combine above and chill.

Serves: 6

Nutrition per serving
Calories	118
Protein	5 g.
Carbohydrate	16 g.
Cholesterol	2 mg.
Sodium	128 mg.
Dietary Fiber	.5 g.

Exchanges
1 1/2 fruit
1/2 meat

ORANGE
JELL-O SALAD

ingredients: 1 large package sugar free orange Jell-o
(use powdered form of Jell-o)
8 oz. non fat cottage cheese
8 oz. fat free Cool Whip
1 cup canned mandarin oranges, drained

directions: Combine above and chill.

Serves: 6

Nutrition per serving

Calories	132
Protein	10 g.
Carbohydrate	38 g.
Cholesterol	2 mg.
Sodium	141 mg.
Dietary Fiber	.7 g.

Exchanges
1/2 meat
1 3/4 fruit

HONEY-YOGURT SALAD DRESSING

ingredients: 1 cup plain non fat yogurt
2 t. honey
1/4 t. ground nutmeg

directions: In a small bowl, mix together all ingredients.
Store in tightly covered jar and refrigerate.
Shake before each serving.

Serves: 4

Nutrition per serving
Calories	43
Protein	3 g.
Carbohydrate	7 g.
Cholesterol	1 mg.
Sodium	44 mg.
Dietary Fiber	0 g.

Exchanges
1/2 milk

CREAMY
GARLIC DRESSING

ingredients: 1 cup plain non fat yogurt
1 1/2 t. fat free Dijon or spicy brown mustard
1/2 t. grated lemon rind
1/8 t. cayenne pepper
2 T. minced parsley
1 minced clove of garlic

directions: Blend the first four ingredients together.
Stir in parsley and garlic.
Cover and chill overnight.

Serves: 4

Nutrition per serving

Calories	41
Protein	4 g.
Carbohydrate	6 g.
Cholesterol	1 mg.
Sodium	101 mg.
Dietary Fiber	.2 g.

Exchanges
1/2 milk

FANTASTIC FRUIT SALAD (IN SEASON)

ingredients: 2 peaches, cut up
1 cup blueberries
1 cup melon balls
3 plums, cut up
1 cup sliced strawberries
1 cup seedless grapes
6 apricots, cut up
2 red apples, cut up
3 bananas, cut up

Fruit Salad Dressing

ingredients: 1 cup fat free plain yogurt
3 T. orange juice
1 orange, peeled (seedless)

directions: Mix dressing in blender until creamy.
Add to fruit in bowl or serve on the side.

Absolutely light, lean, and luxurious!

Serves: 8

Nutrition per serving		Exchanges
Calories	157	2 1/2 fruit
Protein	4 g.	1/2 milk
Carbohydrate	37 g.	
Cholesterol	1 mg.	
Sodium	32 mg.	
Dietary Fiber	5 g.	

SPINACH AND
SPROUTS SALAD

ingredients: 1 cup brussels sprouts
2 cups cauliflower pieces
1 cup spinach, torn into bite size pieces

Spinach and Sprouts Dressing

ingredients: 1/2 cup fat free cottage cheese
1/4 cup red wine vinegar
1 T. lemon juice
1/2 t. salt substitute
1/4 t. dry mustard
1/4 t. pepper

directions: Mix brussels sprouts, cauliflower
and dressing together.
Refrigerate for 1 hour.
Take it out of the refrigerator and
toss with spinach and serve.

Serves: 2

Nutrition per serving		Exchanges
Calories	93	3 vegetable
Protein	11 g.	1/2 meat
Carbohydrate	15 g.	
Cholesterol	3 mg.	
Sodium	239 mg.	
Dietary Fiber	5.2 g.	

NATURE'S SALAD

ingredients: 1/2 head iceberg lettuce
1/2 cup mushrooms, sliced
1 cup alfalfa sprouts
1 cup bean sprouts

directions: Mix the salad together and refrigerate.

Nature's Dressing

ingredients: 1/2 cup fat free cottage cheese
1/2 cup fat free Alpine Lace Parmesan Cheese

directions: Blend fat free cottage cheese in the
blender until creamy.
Add Fat Free Alpine Lace Parmesan Cheese
to the top of the Nature's salad and serve.

Absolutely delicious!

Serves: 2

Nutrition per serving		Exchanges
Calories	137	3 vegetable
Protein	19 g.	1 meat
Carbohydrate	17 g.	
Cholesterol	22 mg.	
Sodium	372 mg.	
Dietary Fiber	3.5 g.	

TOSSED GREEN SALAD

ingredients: 1/2 head iceberg lettuce
2 hard boiled egg whites
1/2 cup mushrooms, sliced
1 small cauliflower, separated
1 medium green pepper, chopped
1/2 cup pimientos
1/2 cucumber, sliced

directions: Toss salad together and refrigerate.

Tossed Green Salad Dressing

ingredients: 1/2 cup cottage cheese (fat free)
2 T. fat free Italian dressing
1 T. onion
1/2 t. pepper

directions: Blend cottage cheese in the blender.
Take it out after smooth and creamy.
Add it to the Fat Free Italian dressing,
onion, and pepper.

Enjoy!

Serves: 2

Nutrition per serving		Exchanges
Calories	117	4 vegetable
Protein	14 g.	1/2 meat
Carbohydrate	18 g.	
Cholesterol	2 mg.	
Sodium	494 mg.	
Dietary Fiber	4.3 g.	

EXCITING EGGS

VERY "UNFRENCH" FRENCH TOAST

ingredients: 6 slices non fat sourdough bread
1 cup Egg Beaters
1/4 t. cinnamon
1/4 t. vanilla
1 pint fresh strawberries
1/2 cup unsweetened natural apple juice
Pam

directions: Combine all ingredients (except bread and Pam) in shallow bowl.
Dip each bread slice in Egg Beaters until coated evenly.
Set aside.
Spray pan with Pam and heat (medium heat).
Place 2 slices of bread in pan at a time and cook until lightly browned.
Meanwhile, wash and hull strawberries.
Blend berries with apple juice until pureed.
Pour over toast and serve immediately.

Serves: 6

Nutrition per serving

		Exchanges
Calories	82	1/2 bread
Protein	5 g.	1/2 fruit
Carbohydrate	17 g.	
Cholesterol	0 mg.	
Sodium	163 mg.	
Dietary Fiber	3.7 g.	

51

ITALIAN VEGGIE AND WHOLE GRAIN EGG WHITE OMELET

ingredients:
Natural Butter Flavor Pam
1/2 medium onion
3-4 cloves garlic
1 diced Roma tomato
1/2 cup diced zucchini
1/2 cup cooked fat free rice
1/4 cup cooked barley
5 egg whites
sprinkle generously with freshly ground pepper, basil, sea salt, and oregano

directions:

Saute in Natural Butter Flavor Pam above ingredients. Set aside a minute.
Respray pan and pour in 5 large egg whites, whipped.
Let cook and flop like a large pancake when able.
Place saute filling on one side and fold 1/2 of egg white over.
Remove from pan in about 1 minute.

Serves 2

Nutrition per serving		Exchanges
Calories	147	1 vegetable
Protein	12 g.	1 bread
Carbohydrate	25 g.	1 meat
Cholesterol	0 mg.	
Sodium	282 mg.	
Dietary Fiber	2.4 g.	

Mary Michaelson, B.S., C.P.F.T., C.S.C.S., Certified Personal Fitness Trainer, Member: ACSM, IDEA, NASM, NSCA. From Scottsdale, AZ.

FRIED MATZO

ingredients: 3 Dietetic Matzo-thins Manischewitz pieces of matzo
1/2 cup Fleischmann's Egg Beaters

directions: Break up the matzo in a large bowl into bite size
pieces.
Wet it with water and then drain the water.
Mix the Egg Beaters with the matzo.
Spray a large frying pan with Pam.
Put matzo mixture in pan and spray it with Pam.
Fry at meduim high, turning frequently.
Continue to spray matzo with Pam every time
it is turned.

Serve plain, with salt, or with jelly.

Serves: 2

Nutrition per serving		Exchanges
Calories	193	1 3/4 bread
Protein	8 g.	1 meat
Carbohydrate	38 g.	
Cholesterol	0 mg.	
Sodium	86 mg.	
Dietary Fiber	1.3 g.	

*Jacie Levy, St. Louis, Missouri. Principal of Craig Elementary
School in the Parkway School District. I am a "fat-free" believer
and user and stay in shape by using the StairMaster and Lifecycle.*

VEGGIE
EGG BEATER OMELET

ingredients: 2 slices fat free cheese
1 cup Egg Beaters
1 chopped tomato
1 chopped green pepper
salt and pepper

directions: Spray frying pan with Pam.
Saute vegetables.
Add Egg Beaters.
Cook until almost set.
Add cheese, cook until melted.
Invert half of omelet.

Serves: 2

Nutrition per serving

		Exchanges
Calories	103	1 meat
Protein	13 g.	2 vegetable
Carbohydrate	13 g.	
Cholesterol	5 mg.	
Sodium	496 mg.	
Dietary Fiber	1.3 g.	

SWISS CHEESE OMELET

ingredients: 1/2 cup Egg Beaters (equivalent to 2 eggs)
2 slices fat free Swiss cheese
Pam

directions: Spray frying pan with Pam.
Add Egg Beaters.
Cook until almost done.
Add fat free Swiss cheese.
Cook until melted.

* For a fabulous variety you may add sauteed mushrooms.

Absolutely mouthwatering! You'll really enjoy this omelet for breakfast or dinner.

Serves: 1

Nutrition per serving
Calories	110
Protein	17 g.
Carbohydrate	11 g.
Cholesterol	10 mg.
Sodium	810 mg.
Dietary Fiber	0 g.

Exchanges
2 meat

Mary Michaelson, B.S., C.P.F.T., C.S.C.S., Certified Personal Fitness Trainer, Member: ACSM, IDEA, NASM, NSCA. From Scottsdale, AZ.

STIR-FRIED VEGGIE OMELET

ingredients: 2 cups broccoli flowers
2 cups cauliflower
2 cups sliced mushrooms
1 potato
2 cups Egg Beaters
4 pieces of fat free Swiss or cheddar cheese
(I personally use both)

directions: First, cook potato for 8 minutes in the microwave.
When it is done, cut it up and put it aside.
Coat wok or large skillet with non stick
cooking spray.
Heat to 300 degrees for a few minutes.
Add first 3 ingredients and stir fry for 2 minutes.
Add the baked potato and blend it in with
the other veggies.
Cook until tender and delicious.
Add Egg Beaters and cheese to the tender veggies.
Cook and then flip to cook the other side.

Absolutely awesome!!

Serves: 4

Nutrition per serving		Exchanges
Calories	146	1 vegetable
Protein	17 g.	2 meat
Carbohydrate	21 g.	
Cholesterol	5 mg.	
Sodium	521 mg	
Dietary Fiber	4.4 g.	

VIGOROUS
VEGETABLES

GLAZED CARROTS

ingredients: 3/4 cup water
8 medium carrots (peeled and sliced diagonally,
1/2 inch thick)
1 cinnamon stick
3/4 t. ground cumin
1/2 t. ginger
1/4 t. ground coriander
1/8 t. cayenne pepper
2 t. honey
2 t. lemon juice

directions: Bring water to boil in heavy 10 inch skillet.
Add next six ingredients.
Cover and simmer (liquid boiling gently) for
12 minutes.
Add honey and lemon juice.
On high heat, boil, until all liquid is gone and carrots
are tender - about 5 minutes.

Serves: 4

Nutrition per serving

Calories	85
Protein	2 g.
Carbohydrate	21 g.
Cholesterol	0 mg.
Sodium	52 mg.
Dietary Fiber	6.3 g.

Exchanges
2 vegetable
1/2 fruit

STEAMED CABBAGE

ingredients: 1 head green cabbage (1 1/2 pounds)
1/2 cup fat free Italian salad dressing

directions: Cut cabbage into wedges.
Sprinkle with salad dressing.
Place in a microwave-proof casserole.
Cover.
Microwave on high for 7 minutes.

Serves: 4

Nutrition per serving

Calories	53
Protein	2 g.
Carbohydrate	17 g.
Cholesterol	0 mg.
Sodium	451 mg.
Dietary Fiber	0 g.

Exchanges
2 vegetable

CAULIFLOWER

ingredients: 1 1/2 cups skim milk
2 cloves minced garlic
1 T. chopped parsley
1 medium head cauliflower
2 t. fresh lemon juice
Pam

directions: Place whole cauliflower in saucepan.
Add milk and bring to a boil.
Reduce heat and simmer until tender - 20 minutes.
Spray Pam in the second saucepan.
Add garlic, parsley and lemon juice to the second saucepan and sauté.
Pour over cauliflower.

Serves: 4

Nutrition per serving

Calories	44
Protein	4 g.
Carbohydrate	7 g.
Cholesterol	2 mg.
Sodium	59 mg.
Dietary Fiber	.8 g.

Exchanges

1/4 milk
1 vegetable

ASPARAGUS

ingredients: 1 pound of asparagus

directions: Wash.
Break off tough ends.
Place in glass oven-proof baking dish with no
additional water, and cover tightly with
aluminum foil.
Bake in oven 15 to 20 minutes at 400°.

Serves: 4

Nutrition per serving	
Calories	26
Protein	3 g.
Carbohydrate	5 g.
Cholesterol	0 mg.
Sodium	3 mg.
Dietary Fiber	2.4 g.

Exchanges
1 vegetable

GREEN BEANS WITH MOZZARELLA AND MUSHROOMS

ingredients: 3 pounds tender young green beans
vinaigrette:
3/4 cup non fat Italian dressing
6 T. fat free Dijon mustard
chopped Italian parsley
1/4 cup sherry
1/4 cup rice vinegar
salt and freshly ground pepper to taste
1/2 pound non fat mozzarella, grated
1/2 pound white mushrooms, trimmed
and sliced thinly

directions: Blanch and chill the beans.
Mix the vinaigrette, whisking or shaking it
until creamy.
Toss the beans with the vinaigrette until
completely coated.
Toss in the mozzarella and mushrooms.

Serves: 6

Nutrition per serving		Exchanges
Calories	186	3 vegetable
Protein	16 g.	1 1/2 meat
Carbohydrate	29 g.	1/2 starch
Cholesterol	6 mg.	
Sodium	1078 mg.	
Dietary Fiber	8.2 g.	

MUSHROOM DELIGHT

ingredients: 12 mushrooms
garlic powder
2 T. fat free cracker or bread crumbs
1 T. chopped parsley
1/4 t. onion powder
1 egg white
Pam

directions: Remove stems from mushrooms, trim ends and chop fine.
Add all ingredients except egg.
Beat egg white until frothy.
Mix with chopped mushroom and spoon egg mixture into mushroom.
Spray Pam on pan.
Bake 20 minutes at 400°.

Serves: 3

Nutrition per serving

Calories	32
Protein	3 g.
Carbohydrate	5 g.
Cholesterol	0 mg.
Sodium	27 mg.
Dietary Fiber	1.1 g.

Exchanges
1 vegetable

STEAMED ARTICHOKE

ingredients: 1 artichoke
2 T. fat free sour cream
dash lemon juice
1 T. horseradish

directions: Steam artichoke for 30 minutes (low heat) after water has boiled.
Combine remaining ingredients for a dip.

Serves: 1

Nutrition per serving
Calories	86
Protein	6.3 g.
Carbohydrate	14 g.
Cholesterol	0 mg.
Sodium	299 mg.
Dietary Fiber	4 g.

Exchanges
2 vegetable

ARTICHOKE CHEESE SQUARES

ingredients:
8 egg whites
1 garlic clove, crushed
1 can artichoke hearts packed in water,
drained and chopped
1/4 cup dry bread crumbs (whole wheat preferably)
1 cup grated non fat cheddar cheese
2 T. chopped parsley
2 T. dehydrated onion flakes
1/2 t. Spike
2 T. fresh basil
dash of pepper
dash of tabasco

directions:
Spray 9 by 9 pan.
Beat whites until foamy and stir in all ingredients.
Pour into dish.
Cook at 325° for 25 minutes.
Let cool and cut into squares.

Note: These are great made a few days earlier
and reheated.

Serves: 6

Nutrition per serving		Exchanges
Calories	53	1 vegetable
Protein	7 g.	1/2 meat
Carbohydrate	6 g.	
Cholesterol	1 mg.	
Sodium	127 mg.	
Dietary Fiber	1.3 g.	

ROASTED PEPPERS "ITALIANO"

ingredients: 6 red peppers
1 cup wine vinegar
salt and pepper to taste
2 T. fresh diced basil

directions: Wash the peppers.
Preheat broiler.
Char peppers at close heat until completely
blackened (turn frequently).
Submerge in cold, salted water and peel off skins,
keeping peppers intact.
Rinse and place in shallow glass pan.
Pour red wine vinegar, salt and pepper over top.
Sprinkle diced fresh basil over top.
Cover and refrigerate.

Serve one pepper per person as an appetizer
or side salad.

Serves: 6

Nutrition per serving		**Exchanges**
Calories	29	1 vegetable
Protein	1 g.	
Carbohydrate	8 g.	
Cholesterol	0 mg.	
Sodium	2 mg.	
Dietary Fiber	2 g.	

STUFFED
CHERRY TOMATOES

ingredients: 16 firm cherry tomatoes
1 small carrot, peeled and grated
2 scallions, sliced
1 medium zucchini, grated
1 celery stalk, chopped
1/4 cup non fat dressing (herb and garlic)

directions: Wash and core the tomatoes.
Put the vegetables in a bowl, toss with the dressing, and carefully fill the tomatoes.
Refrigerate until serving time.

Serves: 4

Nutrition per serving

Calories	52
Protein	2 g.
Carbohydrate	14 g.
Cholesterol	0 mg.
Sodium	240 mg.
Dietary Fiber	2.9 g.

Exchanges
2 vegetable

GREEN BEAN SURPRISE

ingredients: 1 pound green beans
2 ripe tomatoes
2 onions (cut lengthwise)
1 cup tomato sauce
1/2 cup water
salt & pepper to taste

directions: Saute onions (spray pan with Pam)
Add beans (tips cut off), tomatoes (cut in small
wedges), tomato sauce and water.
Salt and pepper to taste
Cover and cook on medium heat until tender.

Serves: 4

Nutrition per serving

Calories	81
Protein	4 g.
Carbohydrate	18 g.
Cholesterol	0 mg.
Sodium	658 mg.
Dietary Fiber	6.4 g.

Exchanges
3 vegetable

SCRUMPTIOUS
SIDE DISHES

VEGETABLE RICE TERIYAKI

ingredients: 1 cup Brown Bran Rice
1/4 cup Teriyaki (your favorite kind)
My favorite kind (if living in Arizona)
is, Shogun's special Teriyaki Sauce. Awesome!

directions: Follow the directions on the brown rice package.
Then add teriyaki sauce.
Extremely simple, but delicious.

Serves: 1

Nutrition per serving

Calories	280
Protein	8 g.
Carbohydrate	62 g.
Cholesterol	0 mg.
Sodium	1920 mg.
Dietary Fiber	0 g.

Exchanges
4 1/2 bread

VEGGIE CASSEROLE

ingredients: 10 oz. frozen package of French style green beans
10 oz. frozen package of broccoli
4 oz. can mushrooms (or fresh)
1/2 cup diced onions
garlic powder to taste

directions: Saute onions in water.
Add pepper and garlic powder to taste.
Cook frozen vegetables as directed.
Combine vegetables and remaining ingredients in casserole and heat in oven or microwave.

Serves: 4

Nutrition per serving

Calories	54
Protein	4 g.
Carbohydrate	11 g.
Cholesterol	0 mg.
Sodium	216 mg.
Dietary Fiber	5 g.

Exchanges
2 vegetable

STUFFED POTATOES

ingredients: 4 potatoes
1 cup skim milk
2 T. Butter Buds
1 T. fat free sour cream

directions: Bake potatoes - 350° for 1 hour.
Let cool a little.
Scoop out inside and put into a bowl.
Mix skim milk, Butter Buds and
sour cream Bet of Butter.

Serves: 4

Nutrition per serving
Calories	121
Protein	5 g.
Carbohydrate	24 g.
Cholesterol	3 mg.
Sodium	166 mg.
Dietary Fiber	1.8 g.

Exchanges
1 starch
1/2 milk

SPANISH RICE

ingredients:
1 cup chopped onions
1 cup chopped green pepper
1 garlic clove
2 2/3 cup uncooked fat free rice
1 can whole tomatoes or Mexican stewed tomatoes
2 t. chili powder
pepper to taste

directions:
Spray Pam in skillet.
Saute onions, green pepper and garlic.
Set aside.
Follow directions for rice.
Add sauteed ingredients and mix with tomatoes,
chili powder and pepper to taste.
Heat through.

Serves: 8

Nutrition per serving		Exchanges
Calories	220	2 bread
Protein	5 g.	2 vegetable
Carbohydrate	51 g.	
Cholesterol	0 mg.	
Sodium	255 mg.	
Dietary Fiber	1.2 g.	

HERBED RICE

ingredients:
2 cups water
1/2 cup shredded carrot
1/2 cup sliced celery
1/3 cup chopped onion
2 t. instant chicken bouillon granules
dash pepper
2/3 cup fat free rice
1 T. snipped parsley

directions:
In medium sauce pan, combine water, carrots, celery, onion, bouillon and pepper.
Bring to boil.
Add uncooked rice.
Return to boiling and reduce heat.
Cover and simmer 20 minutes or until rice is tender.
Remove from heat, let stand 5 minutes and fluff with a fork.
Stir in parsley.

Serves: 2

Nutrition per serving		Exchanges
Calories	232	2 bread
Protein	5 g.	3 vegetable
Carbohydrate	53 g.	
Cholesterol	0 mg.	
Sodium	77 mg.	
Dietary Fiber	2 g.	

RICE TERIYAKI

ingredients: 1 1/3 cup uncooked fat free rice
8 oz. mixed vegetables
1/2 cup low sodium teriyaki sauce

directions: Cook rice according to package directions
(NO margarine).
Cook vegetables according to package directions.
Drain vegetables.
Add vegetables to rice.
Add teriyaki sauce to taste.

Serves: 4

Nutrition per serving

Calories	286
Protein	8 g.
Carbohydrate	64 g.
Cholesterol	0 mg.
Sodium	987 mg.
Dietary Fiber	3.1 g.

Exchanges

2 bread
1 vegetable

SLICED POTATOES

ingredients: 3 potatoes sliced
1 t. chopped garlic
1 1/2 cups grated fat free cheese
3/4 cup skim milk
salt and pepper to taste

directions: Spray casserole with a good coating of Pam.
Arrange potatoes in casserole alternately with cheese and salt and pepper.
Pour milk around edges.
Bake about one hour at 400°.

Serves: 6

Nutrition per serving

Calories	140
Protein	16 g.
Carbohydrate	20 g.
Cholesterol	15 mg.
Sodium	921 mg.
Dietary Fiber	.9 g.

Exchanges

1 starch
1/4 milk
1 meat

POTATOES
AU VEGGIES

ingredients: 1 1/3 cups instant mashed potatoes
1/3 cup skim milk
salt and pepper
8 oz. frozen mixed vegetables

directions: Cook potatoes according to directions on package, omitting margarine and adding a touch extra milk. Cook vegetables according to directions on package and drain.
Add veggies to potatoes.

Serves: 4

Nutrition per serving

Calories	114
Protein	5 g.
Carbohydrate	25 g.
Cholesterol	0 mg.
Sodium	57 mg.
Dietary Fiber	3.1 g.

Exchanges
1 1/2 vegetable
1 starch

NOODLE CHEESE PUDDING

ingredients: 1 cup fat free egg substitute
1 cup fat free sour cream
2 T. sugar
2 cups nonfat cottage cheese
5 cups cooked pasta
4 T. fat free cornflake crumbs

directions: Preheat oven to 375 degrees.
Combine egg substitute, sour cream, and sugar and beat well.
Stir in cheese and noodles.
Lightly spray a 2 quart pan with cooking spray and place noodle mixture in pan.
Sprinkle with cornflake crumbs.
Bake 40 minutes.

Serves: 6

Nutrition per serving

Calories	284
Protein	20.2 g.
Carbohydrate	48.6 g.
Cholesterol	3 mg.
Sodium	331 mg.
Dietary Fiber	1.5 g.

Exchanges
2 meat
2 bread

HASH BROWNS

ingredients: 4 medium size potatoes
1 onion
Pam

directions: Cut potatoes into cube size pieces.
Cut onion into small pieces.
Spray brownie tin with Pam.
Place cut potatoes and onions on pan and spray with Pam.
Bake at 350° for 20 minutes, then put into broiler until golden brown.

Serves: 4

Nutrition per serving

Calories	96
Protein	3 g.
Carbohydrate	22 g.
Cholesterol	0 mg.
Sodium	144 mg.
Dietary Fiber	2.3 g.

Exchanges

1 starch
1/2 vegetable

Betty and Bill Levy, St. Louis, Missouri.
"We believe in Fat Free Living."

"I CAN'T BELIEVE IT'S FAT FREE FRIES"

ingredients: 4 medium size Idaho russet potatoes
Pam

directions: Cut potatoes into French fry size pieces.
Spray cookie sheet (or brownie pan) with Pam.
Place cut potatoes on pan and spray with Pam.
Bake at 350° for 20 minutes, then put into broiler
until golden brown.

Serves: 4

Nutrition per serving
(without Pam)

Calories	88	
Protein	2 g.	
Carbohydrate	20 g.	
Cholesterol	0 mg.	
Sodium	7 mg.	
Dietary Fiber	1.8 g.	

Exchanges

1 starch

Betty and Bill Levy, St. Louis, Missouri.
"We believe in Fat Free Living."

SPANISH RICE

ingredients: 2 cups cooked fat free rice
1/2 cup salsa

directions: Make rice according to package except for
1/2 of water.
Add salsa instead.

Serves: 2

Nutrition per serving

Calories	220
Protein	4 g.
Carbohydrate	50 g.
Cholesterol	0 mg.
Sodium	640 mg.
Dietary Fiber	0 g.

Exchanges

2 1/2 bread
1 vegetable

*Christine Griebel, CHEC. , Health Educator, H.E.R.O. Life
Management Program SAFA President, Certified Aerobic Instructor
at E1 Conquistador Country Club in Tucson, Arizona,
Mother of 3 boys*

STUFFING

ingredients:
1 medium onion, chopped
3 stalks celery, chopped
1-2 t. poultry seasoning or sage
1/2 t. salt
pinch parsley (optional)
5 cups fat free Kellogg's croutettes
1/3 cup liquid Butter Buds
5 large mushrooms, finely chopped
Pam

directions:
Saute onion, celery and mushrooms in Pam.
Mix remaining ingredients together in oven-safe,
Pammed dish.
Add sauteed ingredients.
Cook at 325 degrees for 45 minutes or until top
is lightly browned.

Serves: 4

Nutrition per serving		Exchanges
Calories	168	2 bread
Protein	6 g.	1/2 vegetable
Carbohydrate	29 g.	
Cholesterol	6 mg.	
Sodium	1233 mg.	
Dietary Fiber	1.3 g.	

Jacie Levy, St. Louis, Missouri.

POTATO SNACK

ingredients: 1 medium potato
diet Hidden Valley Dry Ranch Dip
Spike

directions: Slice potato into thin slices.
Pour other ingredients on potato.
Microwave on high for approximately 6 minutes
or until slices are tender.

Serves: 1

Nutrition per serving		**Exchanges**
Calories	93	1 starch
Protein	2 g.	
Carbohydrate	21 g.	
Cholesterol	0 mg.	
Sodium	327 mg.	
Dietary Fiber	1.8 g.	

PARSLEY POTATOES

ingredients: 4 medium potatoes
1 T. seasoning salt
1 T. parsley flakes
4 t. Butter Buds

directions: Wash and slice potatoes 1/4 ".
Spread out in shallow baking dish and add
1/4 cup water.
Sprinkle with seasoning salt and parsley flakes.
Cover with Saran Wrap and cook in microwave
on high for 5 minutes.
Flip potatoes over.
Sprinkle with Butter Buds.

Serves: 4

Nutrition per serving
Calories	100
Protein	3 g.
Carbohydrate	21 g.
Cholesterol	1 mg.
Sodium	1121 mg.
Dietary Fiber	2 g.

Exchanges
1 1/4 starch

Debbie Harris

BAKED POTATOES WITH CREAMY CUCUMBER SAUCE

ingredients:
32 oz. non fat yogurt
2 cucumbers, peeled and grated
5-6 garlic cloves
1 t. dried dill weed
salt and pepper to taste

directions:
Mix above ingredients and serve over baked potatoes.

Serves: 8

Nutrition per serving
(without potatoes)

Calories	77
Protein	7 g.
Carbohydrate	12 g.
Cholesterol	2 mg.
Sodium	89 mg.
Dietary Fiber	.6 g.

Exchanges

1 vegetable
1/2 milk

Mary Dingeldein is the service manager for
Bally's Vic Tanny Health Club in Madison, Wisconsin

SWEET POTATOES

ingredients: 1 medium sweet potato
1 T. diet maple syrup

directions: Poke several fork holes in potato.
Microwave sweet potato on high for 6 minutes
or until tender.
Serve with maple syrup.

Serves: 1

Nutrition per serving

Calories	169
Protein	2 g.
Carbohydrate	40 g.
Cholesterol	0 mg.
Sodium	56 mg.
Dietary Fiber	3.9 g.

Exchanges
2 starch

CREAMY CABBAGE

ingredients: 3 cups cabbage, shredded
1/3 cup onion, chopped fine
1/3 cup cucumber, chopped finely

Dreamy Dressing

ingredients: 2/3 cup nonfat cottage cheese
1 pack Sweet 'N Low
2 t. red wine vinegar
1 T. skim milk
1/2 t. salt substitute

directions: Mix salad together and refrigerate.
In blender, blend cottage cheese until creamy.
Add other ingredients.
Mix into salad and serve.

Fabulous!

Serves: 2

Nutrition per serving		Exchanges
Calories	90	2 vegetable
Protein	12 g.	1 meat
Carbohydrate	12 g.	
Cholesterol	3 mg.	
Sodium	259 mg.	
Dietary Fiber	3 g.	

BRAVO BREADS

GARLIC CHEESE BREAD

ingredients: 12 slices sourdough bread
1 1/2 cups Alpine Lace Mozzarella grated cheese
6 slices Kraft fat free American cheese
6 t. garlic powder
12 t. Molly McButter

directions: Shake Molly McButter on bread.
Add both cheeses and garlic powder.
Broil until brown.

Serves: 12

Nutrition per serving
Calories	71
Protein	6 g.
Carbohydrate	12 g.
Cholesterol	5 mg.
Sodium	375 mg.
Dietary Fiber	2.5 g.

Exchanges
1/2 starch
1/2 meat

CRUNCHY
BLUEBERRY MUFFINS

ingredients: 2 cups flour
1/2 cup sugar
1 T. baking powder
1/2 t. salt or substitute
1/2 t. cinnamon
1/2 cup cholesterol free egg substitute
1 1/4 cup non fat sour cream
1/4 cup Karo syrup
1 cup wheat and barley cereal (grape-nut)

directions: Blend flour, sugar, baking powder, cinnamon
and salt.
In another bowl, whip egg substitute until foamy.
Add and blend fat free sour cream and syrup.
Mix till blended.
Fold in 1/2 cup of blueberries and cereal.
Pour in lined muffin cups.
Bake at 375° for 25 to 30 minutes.

Yields: 12 muffins

Nutrition per serving		**Exchanges**
Calories	186	2 1/4 starch
Protein	5 g.	
Carbohydrate	42 g.	
Cholesterol	0 mg.	
Sodium	172 mg.	
Dietary Fiber	1 g.	

*Emily McIntyre, Fort Wayne, Indiana, Aerobic Instructor for about
2 1/2 years, mainly teaching step training this session.*

MEXI-CORNBREAD

ingredients:
1 cup flour
1 cup cornmeal
1 cup skim milk
1 t. baking powder
1 small can Mexi-corn
2 egg whites
non-stick cooking spray

directions:
Preheat oven to 400°.
Spray large pan or cast iron corn bread griddle
(I prefer the latter) with non-stick cooking spray.
Drain corn.
Mix all ingredients well.
Bake for 15 to 20 minutes or until golden brown.

Serves: 8

Nutrition per serving

Calories	152
Protein	6 g.
Carbohydrate	31 g.
Cholesterol	1 mg.
Sodium	147 mg.
Dietary Fiber	1.5 g.

Exchanges
2 starch

Yvonne Spencer, Tucson, Arizona, "I just moved to Tucson and had another baby. I plan to start teaching again after the holidays (Jan, 1992). I am a single mother of four and love art."

BRAN MUFFINS

ingredients: 1 cup Egg Beaters (equivalent to 4 eggs)
2 cups skim milk
4 T. honey
4 T. molasses
3 cups bran flakes (cereal)
2 cups whole wheat flour
2 cups oat bran
1/2 cup brown sugar
2 t. baking powder
2 t. baking soda
2 to 3 cups of raisins

directions: Mix in a big bowl. Add 2 to 3 cups raisins (I add the whole box). Mix again carefully. Spray muffin pan with Pam. Bake at 400° for 18 to 20 minutes.

Makes 18 extra large muffins.

Add blueberries if desired. Delicious!

Nutrition per serving		Exchanges
Calories	176	2 starch
Protein	5 g.	1/4 fruit
Carbohydrate	43 g.	
Cholesterol	0 mg.	
Sodium	243 mg.	
Dietary Fiber	2.4 g.	

Jyl Steinback, Phoenix, Arizona. "I am a personal fitness trainer and love working one-on-one. My favorite aerobic workouts are Stairmaster, Lifecycle, rollerblading, climbing mountains and swimming. I love staying in shape and feeling excited about life! I have a wonderful daughter named Jamie who loves swimming and gymnastics, a wonderful son, Scott, who is new to this world, (six months), and loves to move his little body, and a wonderful husband named Gary. He loves mountain biking, weight lifting, and being 5% fat."

BIALY PARMESAN CHEESE BREAD

ingredients: 1 bialy
1 T. Alpine Lace Fat Free Parmesan Cheese
1 t. Butter Buds

directions: Cut the bialy in half horizontally.
Add Butter Buds to both halves.
Sprinkle fat free Parmesan cheese over
the Butter Buds.
Toast for 15 minutes at 350°.
Turn off the oven and let sit for 15 minutes
to turn crispy and fabulous.
Cut into smaller pieces and serve.

Outstanding bread; you will love it!

Serves: 1

Nutrition per serving

Calories	81
Protein	2 g.
Carbohydrate	2 g.
Cholesterol	6 mg.
Sodium	130 mg.
Dietary Fiber	0 g.

Exchanges
1 starch

BANANA BREAD

ingredients: 1/2 cup apple sauce
1 cup sugar (or 1/4 cup sugar, 1/2 cup
sweet and low)
4 egg whites
4 medium bananas (ripe)
2 cups flour
1 t. baking soda
1/2 t. "No Salt"

directions: Cream apple sauce and sugar.
Add egg whites, mash bananas and mix thoroughly.
Sift dry ingredients and add to banana mixture.
Spray bread pan with Pam or Weight Watchers' spray.
Pour mixture into pan.
Bake at 375° for 10 minutes.
Reduce heat to 350° and bake for 35-45 minutes
(best to check at 35 minutes).
Remove from oven and let sit 5 minutes.
Remove from bread pan and let cool on rack.

Serves: 8

Nutrition per serving		Exchanges
Calories	283	1 fruit
Protein	6 g.	2 3/4 starch
Carbohydrate	66 g.	
Cholesterol	0 mg.	
Sodium	187 mg.	
Dietary Fiber	1.6 g.	

Jill Reinke, Scottsdale, Arizona.
Fitness Director at Family Fitness Center.

SPICY MUFFINS

ingredients: 1/2 cup Egg Beaters
1/2 cup fat free sour cream
1/2 cup skim milk
3/4 cup raisins
1 1/2 cups flour
1/2 cup multi-grain Quaker Oats
1/2 cup sugar
2 T. instant coffee
2 t. baking powder
1/2 t. of both cinnamon and Allspice

directions: Put first 3 ingredients into bowl with coffee granules.
Beat until blended.
Add raisins.
Let stand until coffee is dissolved and stir.
Preheat oven to 375°.
Line muffin tin with 12 cupcake papers.
In large bowl, mix spices, baking powder,
sugar and flour.
Add sour cream mixture and use rubber spatula
to blend all ingredients until moistened.
Put batter into cupcake papers.
Bake 25 minutes.

Serves: 12

Nutrition per serving		**Exchanges**
Calories	137	1 starch
Protein	4 g.	1 fruit
Carbohydrate	31 g.	
Cholesterol	0 mg.	
Sodium	82 mg.	
Dietary Fiber	.6 g.	

93

FREE FOR ALL MUFFINS OR LOAF

ingredients: 1 1/2 cups whole wheat flour
1 t. salt
1 1/2 t. baking soda
1 t. cinnamon
1/2 t. nutmeg
1 1/2 cups bran
add 1 cup of vegetables, any fruit (banana, zucchini, carrot, or use combination)
3 egg whites
1 1/2 cups apple juice
2 T. white vinegar
1/2 cup honey
1/4 cup molasses

directions: Blend flour, salt, baking soda, cinnamon, nutmeg and bran in food processor for 5-10 seconds.
Set aside.
Blend choice of fruits and vegetables and add to dry ingredients above.
Add eggs and rest of the ingredients to bowl.
Stir with spoon.
Paper line cups or spray Pam on muffin tin.
Bake muffins at 375° for 20-25 minutes.
Bake loaf at 375° for 35-45 minutes.
Serves: 12

Nutrition per serving		Exchanges
Calories	152	1 1/2 starch
Protein	4 g.	1/2 fruit
Carbohydrate	37 g.	
Cholesterol	0 mg.	
Sodium	357 mg.	
Dietary Fiber	5.5 g.	

Karen Moore, Burnsville, Minnesota

NON FAT
SPICE MUFFINS

ingredients: preheat oven to 400°
1 cup crushed Fiber One
1 cup All Bran, Corn Bran, etc.
1/2 cup multi-grain oatmeal
1 1/2 cup skim milk
4-5 packages Equal
3 egg whites
1/2 - 1 cups chunky applesauce
1/2 cup non fat sour cream
1/2 cup packed brown sugar
vegetable spray
dry mixture:
1 1/2 cups whole wheat flour
3 t. baking powder
1 t. baking soda
2 t. cinnamon
1 t. cardamon
1 t. nutmeg
2 T. wheat germ
1/2 cup grapenuts
1/2 cup raisins

directions: Pour skim milk on top of Fiber One and All Bran.
Let soak and add Equal. Add egg whites, applesauce,
sour cream and brown sugar: if not moist enough,
add more nonfat sour cream (1 T. at a time).
Add dry to wet mixture and blend until moist.
Sprinkle in 1/2 cup Grapenuts and 1/2 cup raisins.
Spoon into paper muffin cups or heart shaped pans
sprayed lightly with vegetable spray.
Bake 20 minutes or until toothpick comes out clean.
Serves: 12

Nutrition per serving		Exchanges
Calories	166	2 bread
Protein	7 g.	3/4 fruit
Carbohydrate	38 g.	
Cholesterol	1 mg.	
Sodium	323 mg.	
Dietary Fiber	5.4 g.	

Mary Michaleson, B.S., C.P.F.T., C.S.C.S., Scottsdale, Arizona

TRACY'S
OATMEAL MUFFINS

ingredients:
1 1/2 cups sour skim milk
2 cups multi-grain oats
1 cup whole wheat flour
1 t. baking soda
1 egg white (beaten)
2 T. brown sugar
vegetable spray

directions:
Soak the oats in the sour milk overnight
in a large bowl.
Preheat oven to 400°.
Sift dry ingredients together.
Combine dry ingredients together with beaten
egg white and sugar.
Add to the oats.
Stir lightly just until the batter is mixed.
Drop batter into vegetable sprayed muffin tins,
filling each cup two-thirds full.
Bake 20 minutes.
Makes 12 muffins.

Note: These are simple to make, but the oats need to soak eight hours or so first. Pasteurized milk doesn't exactly sour. So simply add 1 tablespoon of vinegar to 1 1/2 cups skim milk. Let stand 5 minutes.

Nutrition per serving		Exchanges
Calories	73	1 starch
Protein	4 g.	
Carbohydrate	15 g.	
Cholesterol	1 mg.	
Sodium	128 mg.	
Dietary Fiber	2.1 g.	

T. Tallent, Tucson, Arizona

BANANA BREAD

ingredients: have all ingredients at about 70 degrees.
preheat oven to 350°.
sift together:
1 3/4 cups all-purpose flour
2 1/4 t. baking soda
1/2 t. salt
blend until creamy:
1/3 cup applesauce
2/3 cup sugar
dried apricot (optional)
beat in:
1/2 cup Egg Beaters
1 1/4 cups ripe mashed banana pulp

directions:

Add sifted dry ingredients in about 3 parts to the sugar mixture.
Beat the batter after each addition until smooth.
If desired, fold in 1/2 cup chopped dried apricots.
Place batter in sprayed bread pan.
Bake the bread about 45 minutes (I tend to underbake mine).
Don't wait for the bread to turn golden brown as an indicator - without the oil it stays rather pale.
Cool before slicing.

Serves: 8

Nutrition per serving		Exchanges
Calories	211	2 starch
Protein	4 g.	1 fruit
Carbohydrate	49 g.	
Cholesterol	0 mg.	
Sodium	510 mg.	
Dietary Fiber	1 g.	

Kathy Moore, Scottsdale, Arizona. Jazzercise Instructor, Personal Trainer and Lecturer.

BRAN MUFFINS

ingredients:
1 cup wheat flour
2 cups 40% Bran Flakes cereal
1/4 cup corn meal
1/2 t. salt
1 t. baking soda
1 1/4 cup skim milk
1/2 cup molasses
1 cup raisins

directions:
Mix all ingredients well.
Spray muffin tin with Pam or use paper lined muffin cups.
Bake at 325° for 25 minutes.

Makes 12.

Nutrition per serving

		Exchanges
Calories	162	2 bread
Protein	5 g.	
Carbohydrate	40 g.	
Cholesterol	0 mg.	
Sodium	300 mg.	
Dietary Fiber	7.2 g.	

Cathy Traver, Missoula, Montana. "I am currently the Montana State IDEA Representative, teaching kids, disabled, seniors and step aerobics for the past 10 years.

FAT FREE
CRANBERRY BREAD

ingredients:
2 cups flour
1 cup sugar
1/2 t. salt
1/2 t. baking powder
1/2 t. baking soda
2 egg whites

directions:
Sift all together.
Add egg whites.
Add 2 T. applesauce.
2 T. hot water
1/2 cup orange juice
1 cup raw cranberries chipped

Mix.
Bake in a small bread pan or meatloaf dish for
1 hour and 10 minutes at 325°.

Serves: 8

Nutrition per serving

Calories	231
Protein	4 g.
Carbohydrate	53 g.
Cholesterol	0 mg.
Sodium	250 mg.
Dietary Fiber	.6 g.

Exchanges
3 bread

FAT FREE
AND FABULOUS
RAISIN-BRAN BREAD

Made with a bread maker.

ingredients:
2 1/4 cups bread flour
1 T. dry skim milk
1 t. sugar
1 t. salt
1/2 t. cinnamon
2 heaping T. bran
2 heaping T. applesauce
1/2 cup raisins
7/8 cup water
1 t. dry yeast

directions:
Put in bread machine and push light bake.

Mouth watering and delicious!

Serves: 8

Nutrition per serving		Exchanges
Calories	177	2 1/4 bread
Protein	5 g.	
Carbohydrate	38 g.	
Cholesterol	0 mg.	
Sodium	272 mg.	
Dietary Fiber	2 g.	

FAT FREE
AND FANTASTIC
APPLE-OATMEAL-
BRAN BREAD

Made with a bread machine.

ingredients:
2 1/4 cups bread flour
1 T. dry skim milk
1 t. sugar
1 t. salt
1/2 t. cinnamon
1/2 cup multi-grain oatmeal
2 heaping T. bran
2 1/2 heaping T. applesauce
5/8 cup water
1 t. dry yeast

directions:
Put in bread machine and press bake.

Absolutely perfection to your mouth!

Serves: 8

Nutrition per serving

Calories	160
Protein	6 g.
Carbohydrate	33 g.
Cholesterol	0 mg.
Sodium	273 mg.
Dietary Fiber	1.9 g.

Exchanges
2 bread

MAGNIFICENT
MAIN COURSES

FISH MARINADE

ingredients: for 6 pieces

6 oz. can pineapple juice
1/2 t. garlic powder
3/4 t. tabasco
1/6 cup sherry
1/6 cup Maggie
1/3 cup Worcestershire
1/2 t. Kitchen Bouquet
pinch seasoned salt

directions: Marinate fish for at least 24 hours in the refrigerator.

Serves: 6

Nutrition per serving
Calories	35
Protein	0 g.
Carbohydrate	7 g.
Cholesterol	0 mg.
Sodium	154 mg.
Dietary Fiber	0 g.

Exchanges
1/2 fruit

Jacie Levy, St. Louis, Missouri

PASTA WITH RED PEPPER LENTIL SAUCE

ingredients:
1/2 cup dried lentils
4 cups water
2 bay leaves
1 1/2 cups diced onions
2 cloves minced garlic
1 T. dried Basil
1/4 cup + 2 T. red wine
2 cups chopped sweet red bell peppers
1 T. balsamic vinegar
1 T. ground black pepper
6 oz. cooked pasta

directions:
Rinse and sort lentils. Boil 4 cups water.
Add lentils and bay leaves. Simmer until lentils are tender but still shapely. Strain and remove bay leaves. Combine onions, garlic, basil in wine. Chop peppers and add to onions. Stew 25-30 minutes till soft. Transfer to blender all vegetables and puree (do not puree lentils).
Add vinegar, salt and pepper to taste.

Serves: 4.

Nutrition per serving		Exchanges
Calories	209	1 starch
Protein	11 g.	1 vegetable
Carbohydrate	39 g.	
Cholesterol	0 mg.	
Sodium	805 mg.	
Dietary Fiber	11.1 g.	

Christine Griebel, Tucson, Arizona

RICE AND GREEN CHILI

ingredients: 4 cups cooked fat free rice
1 cup plain yogurt
1 small can green chilis
1 cup favorite salsa

directions: Heat oven 350°.
Mix above.
Spray Pam in a baking dish.
Pour in mixture.
Bake 20 minutes.
May be sprinkled with your favorite non fat cheese.

Serves: 4

Nutrition per serving

Calories	263	
Protein	8 g.	
Carbohydrate	57 g.	
Cholesterol	1 mg.	
Sodium	685 mg.	
Dietary Fiber	4.9 g.	

Exchanges

2 3/4 bread
1/4 milk
1 vegetable

Karen Carnow, Phoenix, Arizona

PASTA STIR FRY

ingredients:
1/2 pound cooked pasta
1 cup sliced mushrooms
1 cup diced broccoli
1 cup sliced zucchini
1 cup onion
2 egg whites
cooking spray

directions:
Coat large frying pan with cooking spray.
Stir fry mushrooms, broccoli, zucchini,
and onions until tender.
Toss in pasta, then egg whites
and stir on low until cooked.

Great quick meal!

Serves: 4

Nutrition per serving		Exchanges
Calories	111	1 bread
Protein	6 g.	1 vegetable
Carbohydrate	21 g.	
Cholesterol	0 mg.	
Sodium	185 mg.	
Dietary Fiber	2.5 g.	

*Kim Margold, St. Louis, Missouri, Personal Trainer for
Bally's Vic Tanny and amateur body builder.*

VEGETARIAN CHILI

ingredients: 4 cups kidney beans
1 1/2 t. chili powder
1 1/2 t. ground cumin
2 cups fat free pasta sauce
1 cup chopped onion
1 cup bell pepper
2 whole garlic cloves, minced

directions: Lightly spray a large nonstick skillet with cooking spray and heat over medium-high heat.
Add onion, bell pepper, and minced garlic and cook 5-10 minutes, until vegetables are tender.
Add pasta sauce, chili powder, and cumin and continue to cook until hot.
Add beans, cover skillet, and simmer 5-10 minutes until heated through.

Serves: 4

Nutrition per serving
Calories	174
Protein	10.3 g.
Carbohydrate	34.1 g.
Cholesterol	0 mg.
Sodium	558 mg.
Dietary Fiber	9.2 g.

Exchanges
2 starch
1 vegetable

QUICK AND EASY PASTA DISH

ingredients: 1 pound favorite pasta, cooked
1 pound frozen broccoli
1/2 cup non fat Italian dressing

directions: Cook pasta in boiling water.
Steam broccoli in the Italian dressing.
Combine both.

Can be eaten hot or cold.
You can substitute vegetable or add others.

Less than 10 minutes!

Serves: 6

Nutrition per serving		Exchanges
Calories	134	2 vegetable
Protein	6 g.	1 bread
Carbohydrate	30 g.	
Cholesterol	0 mg.	
Sodium	299 mg.	
Dietary Fiber	3.3 g.	

*Rosie Multari, certified fitness instructor specializing
in seniors and special populations, creator of "Ease to
the Beat" program and video and IDEA New Jersey
State Representative (90 - 94).*

VEGETABLE PIZZA

ingredients: crust:
2 1/2 - 3 cups whole wheat flour
1 package active dry yeast
1/2 cup warm water

sauce:
1 cup tomato paste
1 t. Italian seasoning
1 t. basil
1 t. oregano
1 t. crushed red pepper

directions: Mix together crust and knead 8-10 minutes.
Spread sauce over pizza crust.
Now the fun! Pineapple, mushrooms, asparagus,
broccoli, onions, anything you want!
Load it up!
Bake 350° - 375° until crust is brown.

Fat free cheese is optional (I don't use cheese).

Makes 10 slices

Nutrition per serving

		Exchanges
Calories	132	1 1/4 bread
Protein	6 g.	1 vegetable
Carbohydrate	28 g.	
Cholesterol	0 mg.	
Sodium	21 mg.	
Dietary Fiber	5.5 g.	

Karen Moore, Burnsville, Minnesota

VEGETABLE QUICHE

ingredients: 1 9" pan
1 garlic bud, finely chopped
3 cups chopped mixed veggies
1 1/2 cups grated fat free white cheese
3/4 cup egg beaters, lightly beaten (equivalent to 3 eggs)
1 cup skim milk
1 onion finely chopped

directions: Cook chopped onion and garlic over low heat (beware of scorching).
Add other chopped veggies.
Cook until tender, stirring often.
Spread veggie mix on bottom of pie pan.
Spread 1/2 of cheese and remaining veggie mix, then top with remaining cheese.
Combine milk and eggs and pour over quiche.
Bake in oven 1 hour at 350° or until browned.

Serves: 4

Nutrition per serving		Exchanges
Calories	194	1/2 milk
Protein	28 g.	2 meat
Carbohydrate	23 g.	2 vegetable
Cholesterol	22 mg.	
Sodium	1602 mg.	
Dietary Fiber	2.5 g.	

Rebecca Lunden-Draeger

GARLIC SCALLOPS AND ANGEL HAIR PASTA

---

ingredients: saute in vegetable spray:
1 medium onion
5 cloves of fresh garlic, minced
1 pound scallops, diced or cubed
1-2 cups cut up fresh broccoli florets

in a bowl, mix together:
1 cup non fat sour cream
1/4 cup non fat yogurt
1 T. garlic
dash of skim milk (to thin to desired consistency)

directions: Pour mix over scallops and vegetables.
Simmer.
Top a plate of cooked angel hair pasta ("capelline")
with mixture.

Serves 3.

Nutrition per serving

		Exchanges
Calories	228	3 meat
Protein	31 g.	1 vegetable
Carbohydrate	25 g.	1/2 starch
Cholesterol	34 mg.	
Sodium	465 mg.	
Dietary Fiber	3.1 g.	

Mary Michaelson, Scottsdale, Arizona

SPAGHETTI WITH WHITE SAUCE

ingredients:
8 oz. spaghetti
1/4 cup fat free cottage cheese
3 T. skim milk
Pinch garlic powder
Dash seasoned salt
Dash pepper
Pinch Italian seasoning
Pinch cayenne pepper

directions:
Cook spaghetti following package directions.
Using a blender, mix the rest of the ingredients.
After spaghetti is cooked, combine blended
ingredients with spaghetti and microwave
for 1 minute or until hot.

Serves: 4

Nutrition per serving		Exchanges
Calories	223	2 bread
Protein	9 g.	1 meat
Carbohydrate	43 g.	
Cholesterol	1 mg.	
Sodium	54 mg.	
Dietary Fiber	1.4 g.	

VEGETARIAN FAJITA PITAS

ingredients: 4 fat free pita pockets
3-4 cups chopped vegetables
1 cup sliced mushrooms
1 large onion
1 cup non fat shredded cheese

to garnish:
non fat sour cream
salsa or diced tomatoes

directions: Wrap chopped vegetables, sliced onions
and mushrooms in foil.
Bake at 350° for 45 minutes or until vegetables,
onions and mushrooms are tender.
Add teriyaki or soy sauce.
Fill pita pockets with mixture and top with cheese.
Microwave for 30 seconds to melt cheese.
Add salsa and sour cream if desired.

Serves: 4

Nutrition per serving
Calories	212
Protein	11 g.
Carbohydrate	41 g.
Cholesterol	1 mg.
Sodium	534 mg.
Dietary Fiber	4.3 g.

Exchanges
1 vegetable
2 bread
1/2 meat

FARMER'S CHOP SUEY

ingredients: 1 large non fat cottage cheese (24 oz.) container
2 cucumbers, chopped
2 tomatoes, chopped
6 scallions, chopped
2 stalks celery, chopped
1/2 green pepper, chopped
4 radishes, chopped
1 carrot, finely shredded

directions: Spike to taste.
Mix above and refrigerate 1 hour.
Serve.

Serves: 6

Nutrition per serving
Calories	108
Protein	16 g.
Carbohydrate	13 g.
Cholesterol	5 mg.
Sodium	377 mg.
Dietary Fiber	2.6 g.

Exchanges
1 meat
2 vegetable

SHRIMP SCRAMBLE

ingredients: 1-1/2 cups fat-free egg substitute
3 T. skim milk
1-4 1/2 oz. can shrimp, drained
1/4 t. pepper
1/2 t. prepared mustard
3 bialys, halved

directions: Combine egg substitute and milk in a medium bowl and mix well.
Stir shrimp into egg mixture; add pepper and mustard and mix well.
Toast bialys and keep warm.
Lightly spray a nonstick skillet with cooking spray.
Add egg mixture and cook, stirring lightly with a fork.
When eggs are set and creamy, spoon over bialy halves.
Serve immediately.

Serves: 3

Nutrition per serving

Calories	167	
Protein	15 g.	
Carbohydrate	19 g.	
Cholesterol	74 mg.	
Sodium	260 mg.	
Dietary Fiber	0 g.	

Exchanges

1 1/2 meat
1 starch

PITA PIZZA

ingredients: 8 fat free pita pockets
2 cups fat free spaghetti sauce
8 slices fat free cheese

directions: Slit pita pocket lengthwise.
Toast each half.
Put spaghetti sauce on each piece.
Top with fat free cheese.
Put under broiler or toaster oven until
cheese is melted.
Can be topped with your favorite vegetables.

Serves: 8

Nutrition per serving

Calories	208
Protein	11 g.
Carbohydrate	39 g.
Cholesterol	5 mg.
Sodium	744 mg.
Dietary Fiber	1.5 g.

Exchanges

1 1/2 starch
1 meat
1 vegetable

PIZZA

---

ingredients: 2 fat free pita pockets, cut in half and cut open
1 1/2 T. tomato paste
1 package Sweet 'N Low
pinch Italian seasoning
pinch pepper
pinch garlic powder
3 T. Alpine Lace fat free mozzarella grated cheese

directions: Toast pita pockets.
Combine all ingredients except cheese.
Spread mixture on the pita pocket.
Add both kinds of cheese.
Broil until cheese is melted.

Variation: Saute chopped mushrooms and
onions in Pam.
Add to pita and cheese combination before broiling.

Serves: 2

Nutrition per serving		**Exchanges**
Calories	182	1 starch
Protein	7 g.	1 meat
Carbohydrate	36 g.	
Cholesterol	0 mg.	
Sodium	351 mg.	
Dietary Fiber	1.5 g.	

BIALY PIZZA

ingredients: 4 plain bialys
16 oz. fat free pasta sauce
1 cup sliced mushrooms
1 cup Alpine Lace Fat Free Shredded Cheese
(your favorite kind)

directions: Cut all bialys into halves.
Pour 1 to 2 T. of pizza sauce on each bialy.
Saute mushrooms and add a few to each bialy.
Sprinkle a handful of fat free shredded cheese
on each bialy.
Toast at 350° for 15 minutes or until the cheese
is melted.

Absolutely mouth watering!
You will love this quick meal!

Serves: 4

Nutrition per serving

Calories	121
Protein	4 g.
Carbohydrate	11 g.
Cholesterol	1 mg.
Sodium	420 mg.
Dietary Fiber	2 g.

Exchanges

1 bread
1/2 meat
1/2 vegetable

COLORFUL BAKED ZITI

ingredients: 1 lb. eggplant, cubed
1 large red onion, diced
1 yellow bell pepper, chopped
1 red bell pepper, chopped
32 oz. jar fat free pasta sauce
15 oz. zita, cooked
10 oz. frozen chopped spinach, thawed & drained
1 cup fat free Mozzarella cheese, shredded

directions: Preheat oven to 450 degrees.
Cook ziti according to package directions and drain.
Lightly spray a cookie sheet with cooking spray.
Arrange eggplant, onion, and peppers on cookie
sheet and spray with cooking spray.
Roast vegetables 30 minutes, stirring several times
until browned.
Reduce oven heat to 400 degrees.
In a large bowl, combine cooked ziti, vegetables,
pasta sauce and spinach.
Spread mixture in a 9" x 13" baking dish, lightly
sprayed with cooking spray, and sprinkle Mozzarella
cheese over the top.
Bake 20 minutes or until hot and bubbly.

Nutrition per serving		Exchanges
Calories	170	1 meat
Protein	8 g.	1 starch
Carbohydrate	35 g.	1 vegetable
Cholesterol	1 mg.	
Sodium	424 mg.	
Dietary Fiber	5.6 g.	

BUTTERY GARLIC SPAGHETTI

ingredients:
1 cup cooked spaghetti
1 t. garlic powder
dash seasoned salt
1 t. Molly McButter
1 t. Molly McButter cheese
dash pepper

directions:
Prepare spaghetti according to package directions. Combine spaghetti with other ingredients.

Serves: 2

Nutrition per serving

Calories	109
Protein	4 g.
Carbohydrate	21 g.
Cholesterol	1 mg.
Sodium	86 mg.
Dietary Fiber	0 g.

Exchanges
1 1/4 bread

SPAGHETTI

ingredients: 1 16 oz. package spaghetti
1 32 oz. can fat free spaghetti sauce
pepper to taste

directions: Cook spaghetti according to directions on package.
Drain and add spaghetti sauce.
Add a touch of sugar or Sweet 'N Low
Add pepper and eat while hot!

Serves: 8

Nutrition per serving		**Exchanges**
Calories	255	2 1/2 bread
Protein	9 g.	2 vegetable
Carbohydrate	52 g.	
Cholesterol	0 mg.	
Sodium	373 mg.	
Dietary Fiber	3.2 g.	

SPAGHETTI SAUCE

ingredients: 2 large onions, chopped
3 large green peppers, chopped
2 cloves garlic, minced
8 oz. mushrooms, sliced
Combine in a large stock pot.

Add:
2 T. oregano
2 T. basil
4 bay leaves
1 T. crushed red pepper
3 16 oz. cans tomatoes
3 15 1/2 oz. cans tomato sauce
3 15 1/2 oz. cans tomato paste

directions: Crush tomatoes with back of spoon.
Cover and simmer 3-4 hours.
Divide into serving portions and freeze.
Reheats better each time and much better
than store brands!

Serves: 12

Nutrition per serving		Exchanges
Calories	74	3 vegetable
Protein	3 g.	
Carbohydrate	17 g.	
Cholesterol	0 mg.	
Sodium	488 mg.	
Dietary Fiber	3.9 g.	

JoAnn Bishop, New Mexico Rep: IDEA

POCKET BREAD SANDWICH

ingredients: 4 Kangaroo fat free pocket bread
8 mushrooms
2 stalks of broccoli
2 tomatoes
1 cup alfalfa sprouts
1 cup fat free Alpine Lace shredded cheese
(cheddar or mozzarella)

directions: Clean and slice the mushrooms.
Clean and slice the broccoli.
Clean and slice in small strips the tomato.
Saute the above ingredients with Pam.
Put all the above ingredients in the pocket bread
and add the alfalfa sprouts (a small handful).
Choose the cheese you would like to use,
or use both (which I personally like best).
Stuff the cheese into the pocket bread.
Put the whole pocket bread into the toaster oven
to melt the cheese and to make the pocket
bread crispy.
Awesome!

Serves: 4

Nutrition per serving		Exchanges
Calories	138	1 starch
Protein	8 g.	1/2 meat
Carbohydrate	28 g.	1 vegetable
Cholesterol	1 mg.	
Sodium	194 mg.	
Dietary Fiber	3.6 g.	

CANTALOUPE SURPRISE

ingredients: 1/2 cantaloupe
3 T. fat free Knudson cottage cheese
1/2 cup fat free granola

directions: Cut cantaloupe in small edible squares.
Place 1/4 to 1/2 cantaloupe in bowl.
Put 2 to 3 T. of fat free cottage cheese
on the cantaloupe.
Now, add fat free granola.

Perfect for a light and healthy lunch.

I alternate fat free cottage cheese and fat free yogurt.
Also mouth watering and terrific!

I also love it with a variety of fruits (strawberries,
honeydew melon, bananas, or any combinations).

Serves: 1

Nutrition per serving		Exchanges
Calories	165	1 starch
Protein	9 g.	1/2 meat
Carbohydrate	35 g.	1 fruit
Cholesterol	2 mg.	
Sodium	162 mg.	
Dietary Fiber	2.1 g.	

CREAM OF WHEAT, RAISINS, AND CINNAMON

ingredients: 2 oz. of Cream of Wheat
1/4 cup raisins
1 t. cinnamon

directions: Cook Cream of Wheat as directed on box.
Add raisins.
Add cinnamon.
Mix together and eat while hot!

Wonderful meal on those cold wintery mornings.
One of my all time favorites.

Serves: 1

Nutrition per serving
Calories	321
Protein	6 g.
Carbohydrate	73 g.
Cholesterol	0 mg.
Sodium	151 mg.
Dietary Fiber	4.4 g.

Exchanges
3 starch
1 1/4 fruit

QUAKER QUICK GRITS AND BANANAS

ingredients: 2 oz. of Quaker Quick Grits
1 banana

directions: Cook Quaker Quick Grits as directed on box.
Slice a banana in small narrow pieces.
Add the bananas to the Quick Grits.
Mix together thoroughly.

Absolutely sweet, warm and wonderful!

May add cinnamon if desired.

Serves: 2

Nutrition per serving		Exchanges
Calories	158	1 starch
Protein	3 g.	1 fruit
Carbohydrate	36 g.	
Cholesterol	0 mg.	
Sodium	1 mg.	
Dietary Fiber	1.4 g.	

VEGETARIAN AND FAT FREE CHILI

ingredients: 1 8 oz. can of tomato juice
1 15.5 oz. can of tomatoes
15.5 oz. tomato sauce
15.5 oz. kidney beans
15.5 oz. chili beans
chili powder
1 1/2 cups cooked spaghetti
fat free saltine crackers

directions: In a large pot on the stove, pour in all the above
ingredients (except the spaghetti and crackers).
Bring to a boil for 2 to 3 minutes.
Then put on simmer for 30 minutes.
In a separate pot, bring water to a boil and
add spaghetti.
Cook until tender.
Put the spaghetti on a plate and add the chili on top,
with crackers on the side.

What a wonderful hot and delicious meal!

Serves: 5

Nutrition per serving		Exchanges
Calories	171	2 starch
Protein	17 g.	1 vegetable
Carbohydrate	55 g.	
Cholesterol	0 mg.	
Sodium	569 mg.	
Dietary Fiber	7.5 g.	

SENSATIONAL
SNACKS

SUPER SNACKING

Instead of high-fat snacks, introduce your friends and family to fat free snacking.

*Instead of candy offer frozen grapes, frozen bananas (these are recipes in Fat Free Living under "Snacks"), fat free granola, fat free jello, pudding (chocolate or vanilla), or fruit kabob and dip (found in Fat Free Living under "Snacks").

*Instead of chips offer Pretzenality (Snyder's hard pretzels), air popcorn with pizazz (these are recipes in Fat Free Living under "Snacks"), Fat Free Quaker Butter Popped Corn Cakes (also caramel and white cheddar), or Childers Natural Potato Chips (100% fat free).

*Instead of chocolate chip cookies, substitute with Snack Wells Cinnamon Graham Snack, Devil's Food Cookie Cake, Fat Free Fig Newtons by Nabisco Foods (also Apple Newtons), or Betty Crocker Chiffon Lemon Cake Mix (confetti angel food or white angel food cake), or Entenmann's.

*Instead of ice cream, make a fat free choice by: fruit juice popsicles, fruit ice, health shake (these are recipes in Fat Free Living under "Snacks"), Dryers fat free vanilla, Kemps frozen yogurt, Simple Pleasures Light frozen dairy dessert, Dole sorbet fruit ice, Weight Watchers fat free ice cream or Smuckers frozen dessert Fruitage. But don't forget to top this off with fat free Smucker's Light hot fudge topping and ENJOY!

AIR POPCORN
WITH PIZZAZZ

ingredients: air popper
2 cups plain popcorn (popped)
Mazola no stick cooking spray
1 t. Best of Butter natural cheddar cheese
1 t. Butter Buds

directions: Pop your plain popcorn.
But, as it is falling into the bowl, spray Mazola.
At the same time, sprinkle the cheddar cheese and
Butter Buds onto the popcorn.
You may use one or the other, or both.
Keep reapplying as needed (personally I like lots).

The Mazola helps the cheddar cheese and Butter
Buds stick to the popcorn for extra outstanding taste.

You will love it!

Yields 2 cups cooked popcorn

Nutrition per serving		Exchanges
Calories	73	1 starch
Protein	2 g.	
Carbohydrate	13 g.	
Cholesterol	3 mg.	
Dietary Fiber	2.4 g.	

FROZEN GRAPES

ingredients: 1 lb. fresh grapes

directions: Clean all of the grapes thoroughly.
Take all the grapes off the stems.
Place grapes in a plastic bag and seal tight (so you don't get freezer taste).
Put the bag in the freezer for 24 hours.

Fabulous cool and delicious fat free snack.

Serves: 4

Nutrition per serving
Calories	72
Protein	.7 g.
Carbohydrate	20 g.
Cholesterol	0 mg.
Sodium	2 mg.
Dietary Fiber	1.4 g.

Exchanges
1 1/4 fruit

FROZEN BANANAS

ingredients: 3 to 5 bananas

directions: Peel each banana.
Put each in a separate bag.
Place the bag in the freezer and leave for 24 hours.

When frozen, I like to wrap a paper towel or
napkin around the bottom of the banana for easy
fun snacking.

Nutrition per banana		**Exchanges**
Calories	105	1 1/2 fruit
Protein	1 g.	
Carbohydrate	27 g.	
Cholesterol	0 mg.	
Sodium	1 mg.	
Dietary Fiber	2.7 g.	

FRUIT KABOB
AND DIP

ingredients: 12 fresh strawberries
12 unsweetened, canned pineapple chunks
12 honeydew melon balls

dip:
1/2 cup fresh strawberries
1/2 cup plain non fat yogurt
1 t. honey

directions: Place fruit on cocktail swords or toothpicks,
alternating 2 strawberries, 2 pineapple chunks,
and 2 melon balls on each.
To prepare dip, whirl all ingredients in blender
until smooth.

Serves: 6

Nutrition per serving

Calories	101	
Protein	2 g.	
Carbohydrate	24 g.	
Cholesterol	0 mg.	
Sodium	21 mg.	
Dietary Fiber	2.4 g.	

Exchanges

1 1/4 fruit
1/4 milk

*Kathy Schievelbein. "I am the aerobics program
director/trainer at Northland Fitness Center in
Bloomington, Minnesota. I have been teaching
for 6 years at various community and corporate
clubs and loving it!"*

HEALTH SHAKE

ingredients: 1/2 package frozen strawberries
1 strawberry and 1 banana non fat yogurt
1 cup seltzer water

directions: Throw into blender and serve.

Serves: 2

Nutrition per serving
Calories	193
Protein	13 g.
Carbohydrate	35 g.
Cholesterol	4 mg.
Sodium	176 mg.
Dietary Fiber	1.6 g.

Exchanges
1 1/2 fruit
1 milk

*Laurie Andrews, Regional Coordinator
for Family Fitness Centers in Orange County.
"I love to run (L.A.) marathon past 3 years,
swim, bike, play tennis, and volleyball."*

134

FRUIT JUICE BARS

ingredients: 1 12 oz. can Dole Pure and Light 100% Fruit Juice
My favorite flavors are pineapple, mandarin,
tangerine or mountain cherry.

directions: Mix juice according to directions on can.
Pour into popsicle forms.
Freeze.

This brand of juice contains no added sugars.
Remember to read the labels.

Serves: 4

Nutrition per serving		Exchanges
Calories	180	3 fruit
Protein	0 g.	
Carbohydrate	45 g.	
Cholesterol	0 mg.	
Sodium	45 mg.	
Dietary Fiber	0 g.	

*Linda Smith, Claremont, Oklahoma. Fitness promoter
and mother of two young daughters. Likes to serve her
children nutritious snacks like popsicles, but often finds
the store bought variety full of sugar and expensive.
Her solution: make your own.*

FRUIT ICE

ingredients: 12 oranges
2 lemons
4 bananas (quartered and sliced)
1 large package frozen strawberries
1 large can crushed pineapple (in its own juice)
1 6 oz. can frozen apple juice concentrate
1 6 oz. can frozen pineapple juice concentrate

directions: Squeeze oranges and lemons.
Add bananas, strawberries, pineapple, and juices.
Add enough water to bring mixture to 1 1/2 inches
to top of ice cream freezer.
Pack ice cream freezer with ice and salt (1 cup salt
for each 2 cups of ice).
Churn.
Mixture freezes in 10 to 15 minutes.
Store any leftovers in freezer.

Serves: 12

Nutrition per serving

Calories	175
Protein	3 g.
Carbohydrate	52 g.
Cholesterol	0 mg.
Sodium	5 mg.
Dietary Fiber	5.3 g.

Exchanges
3 fruit

*Linda Smith's favorite summer treat, a recipe
of her father's (the late "Doc" Lacy). He was the best.*

SPECTACULAR SOUPS

BROCCOLI SOUP

ingredients: 1 1/2 cups chopped broccoli (or 10 ounce frozen broccoli)
1/4 cup chopped onion
1 cup fat free chicken broth (or chicken bouillon)
1/4 cup grated Alpine Lace Swiss cheese
2 cups non fat milk
2 T. cornstarch
dash pepper
dash ground thyme

directions: Place vegetables and broth in saucepan.
Bring to a boil.
Reduce heat.
Cover and cook vegetables until they are tender (8 minutes).
Add milk, cornstarch, and pepper.
Stir until soup is slightly thickened and mixture begins to boil.
Remove from heat and add cheese, stirring until melted.

Serves: 4

Nutrition per serving		Exchanges
Calories	98	1 vegetable
Protein	10 g.	1/2 meat
Carbohydrate	15 g.	1/2 milk
Cholesterol	6 mg.	
Sodium	382 mg.	
Dietary Fiber	1.2 g.	

VEGGIE CONSOMME OR STOCK

ingredients: 1 gallon water
1 red onion, cut into wedges
1 brown onion, cut into wedges
3 scallions, sliced
1 potato, thickly sliced
4 celery stalks, thickly sliced
3 carrots, peeled and thickly sliced
2 leeks (white part only), washed and thickly sliced
2 turnips, peeled and cut into wedges
1 zucchini, ends trimmed, thickly sliced
1 red or green pepper, stemmed, seeded,
and cut into chunks
4 tomatoes, seeded and coarsely chopped
3 garlic cloves
2 sprigs Italian parsley
2 bay leaves
1 T. fresh thyme or 1 1/2 t. dried

directions: Put all ingredients in a large stock pot. Bring to boil.
Lower the heat and simmer, uncovered, very slowly
for 2 hours.
Strain the stock, discarding the solids.
Let cool to room temperature.

Substitute this rich stock for any recipe
requiring chicken stock and automatically
make it a non fat meal.

Serves: 12

Nutrition per serving		Exchanges
Calories	87	3 vegetable
Protein	4 g.	
Carbohydrate	19 g.	
Cholesterol	0 mg.	
Sodium	134 mg.	
Dietary Fiber	4.1 g.	

VEGETABLE NOODLE SOUP

ingredients: 4 chicken bouillon cubes
4 cups water
4 cups V8 Juice
2 cups chopped assorted cooked vegetables
1 cup macaroni noodles, cooked

directions: Boil and mix.
Simmer for 1 hour.
Add cooked noodles.

Serves: 4

Nutrition per serving

Calories	117
Protein	5 g.
Carbohydrate	24 g.
Cholesterol	1 mg.
Sodium	2050 mg.
Dietary Fiber	3.7 g.

Exchanges

3 vegetable
1/2 bread

MUSHROOM BARLEY SOUP

ingredients:
1 medium onion, cut in quarters
1 lb. mushrooms
3 T. fat free chicken broth
6 cups water
1/3 cup barley
1/2 t. black pepper
1 whole bay leaf
1/2 t. thyme
2 T. low sodium soy sauce
1/4 cup chopped parsley

directions:
Slice onion and mushrooms in food processor with medium-sized slicer.
Heat chicken broth over high heat in a 3 quart pot. Add onion and cook over medium heat until onion become soft.
Add mushroom and cookover high heat, about 5 minutes, until vegetables are tender.
Add water, barley, pepper, thyme and bay leaf.
Bring soup to a boil; cover and simmer about 45 minutes, until barley is tender.
Stir in soy sauce and simmer another 5 minutes.
Remove bay leaf and stir choppped parsley into soup.
Cook 5 minutes longer and serve hot.

Serves: 6

Nutrition per serving
Calories	64
Protein	3.3 g.
Carbohydrate	12.5 g.
Cholesterol	0 mg.
Sodium	244 mg.
Dietary Fiber	3.2 g.

Exchanges
2 vegetable
1/4 starch

MEXICAN SOUP

ingredients: 4 chicken bouillon cubes
4 cups water
1/2 cup mild salsa
1/2 instant rice

directions: Boil together.
Cover and simmer for 30 minutes.

Serves: 4

Nutrition per serving

Calories	44
Protein	1 g.
Carbohydrate	9 g.
Cholesterol	1 mg.
Sodium	1472 mg.
Dietary Fiber	0 g.

Exchanges
1/2 starch

GAZPACHO SOUP

ingredients: 2 cups tomato juice without salt
1 15.5 oz. can stewed Mexican flavored tomatoes
2 ripe tomatoes, chopped
1/2 red onion, chopped fine
1 green pepper, chopped and seeded
1 cucumber, chopped
1/4 cup red wine vinegar
2 cloves garlic, crushed
2 T. chopped cilantro
1 T. chopped parsley

directions: Blend all of the above.
Chill well.

Can be served with fat free croutons
(look under salads).

Serves: 4

Nutrition per serving

Calories	94
Protein	4 g.
Carbohydrate	22 g.
Cholesterol	0 mg.
Sodium	306 mg.
Dietary Fiber	3.2 g.

Exchanges
4 vegetable

Karen Carnow, Phoenix, Arizona

DELECTABLE DESSERTS

FAT FREE AND FABULOUS YOGURT DESSERT

ingredients: 4 oz. fat free frozen yogurt (your favorite flavor)
2 T. fat free granola
bowl and spoon

directions: Put 4 oz. fat free frozen yogurt in a bowl.
Top it off with your fat free granola.

Super, simple, great crunch and hits the spot!

Serves: 1

Nutrition per serving

Calories	137
Protein	5 g.
Carbohydrate	25 g.
Cholesterol	0 mg.
Sodium	60 mg.
Dietary Fiber	0 g.

Exchanges

1/2 milk
1 bread

ICE CREAM CAKE

ingredients: 2 cups fat free ice cream or yogurt
Entenmann's fat free pound cake

directions: Horizontally slice the cake into three layers.
Smooth ice cream between each layer.
Cut vertically to serve.

Serves: 6

Nutrition per serving
Calories	185
Protein	4 g.
Carbohydrate	41 g.
Cholesterol	0 mg.
Sodium	193 mg.
Dietary Fiber	0 g.

Exchanges
1/2 milk
1 3/4 starch

CHOCOLATE ICE CREAM DELIGHT

ingredients: 1 Entenmann's Fat Free Chocolate Loaf Cake
8 zo. any flavor fat free frozen yogurt
4 oz. fat free Cool Whip

directions: Split cake into 3 layers.
Put 1 pint yogurt between the two layers.
Top with small amount of Cool Whip, covering
the entire top of cake.
Slice and serve.

You will think you're eating lots of fat–it's so
exciting and it is totally fat free!

Serves: 6

Nutrition per serving

Calories	167
Protein	6 g.
Carbohydrate	61 g.
Cholesterol	0 mg.
Sodium	367 mg.
Dietary Fiber	2 g.

Exchanges

1 1/2 starch
1/2 fruit

PEACH DELIGHT

ingredients: 1 angel food cake
1 quart peach ice cream (fat free, of course)
8 oz. fat free Cool Whip
2 peaches, sliced

directions: Slit cake.
Put peach fat free ice cream in between each layer.
Cover with light Cool Whip on top.
Garnish with peach slices.

Variation: Strawberry fat free ice cream
garnish with strawberries.

Variation: Use fat free pound cake.

Serves: 12

Nutrition per serving		Exchanges
Calories	231	1 starch
Protein	5 g.	1/2 milk
Carbohydrate	48 g.	1 3/4 fruit
Cholesterol	0 mg.	
Sodium	286 mg.	
Dietary Fiber	.3 g.	

BANANA
BROWNIE SUNDAE

ingredients: Pam
1/4 cup nonfat dry milk
1 cup all purpose flour
1/3 cup cocoa
1/4 t. baking soda
1/4 t. salt
1 large very ripe banana
1 cup sugar
1 large egg white
1/4 cup skim milk + 1/8 t. lemon juice
1 t. vanilla

directions: Preheat oven to 350°.
Coat 9" baking pan with Pam.
Combine nonfat dry milk, flour, cocoa, soda and salt.
Puree banana in blender; add sugar, egg white, milk
and lemon juice and vanilla until smooth.
Combine dry ingredients with banana,
mix until blended.
Bake 25 minutes.

Serves: 8

Nutrition per serving		Exchanges
Calories	194	1 starch
Protein	5 g.	2 fruit
Carbohydrate	45 g.	
Cholesterol	1 mg.	
Sodium	138 mg.	
Dietary Fiber	1.5 g.	

*Alisa Hall teaches aerobics and has two beautiful
daughters and a son. Alisa is from Claremore, OK.*

APPLE COFFEE CAKE

ingredients:
2 cups all purpose flour
1 1/2 t. baking soda
1/2 t. ground nutmeg
1 cup apple sauce
2 cups sugar
1 t. vanilla extract
1/4 cup Egg Beaters
2 medium Pippin apples, peeled, cored and grated
powdered sugar
Pam

directions:
Preheat oven to 325°.
Spray Pam on a 9 inch bundt pan.
Dust pan with flour; tap out excess.
Mix 2 cups flour, baking soda and nutmeg
in small bowl.
Using electric mixer, mix applesauce with sugar
and vanilla in large bowl until well blended.
Add Egg Beaters.
Add half of dry ingredients and beat well.
Gradually add remaining dry ingredients, beating
well after each addition.
Fold in grated apples.
Spoon batter into prepared pan; smooth top.
Bake until tester inserted near center comes out
clean and top is golden brown, about 70 minutes.
Cool cake in pan on rack 10 minutes.
Turn out onto rack and cool completely.
Sift powdered sugar over and serve.

Serves: 10

Nutrition per serving		Exchanges
Calories	285	3 starch
Protein	3 g.	3/4 fruit
Carbohydrate	69 g.	
Cholesterol	0 mg.	
Sodium	199 mg.	
Dietary Fiber	1.1 g.	

BANANA STRAWBERRY SOUFFLE

ingredients: 1 banana
2 cups chopped strawberries
5 egg whites, beaten
Weight Watcher's Cooking Spray

directions: In non stick skillet sprayed with Weight Watcher's
Cooking Spray, cook egg whites on low heat,
stirring occasionally.
As eggs turn fluffy, add chopped strawberries
and banana.
Use strawberry juice and cinnamon as garnish.

Serves: 2

Nutrition per serving
Calories	139
Protein	10 g.
Carbohydrate	25 g.
Cholesterol	0 mg.
Sodium	139 mg.
Dietary Fiber	4.8 g.

Exchanges
1 1/4 fruit
1 meat

Terry Jones , Paradise Valley, Arizona. Director of
Aerobics at World Gym. She has been teaching and
training other instructors for 10 years. Her certifi-
cations include A.C.E. Gold, A.C.S.M., N.E.A.D.A.
Terry is alsc an A.F.F.A. Examiner .

FLUFFY TAPIOCA PUDDING

ingredients:
1 egg white
1/3 cup sugar or 8 packets of Equal
3 T. tapioca (quick cooking)
2 cups skim milk
1/4 cup fat free Egg Beaters

directions:
Microwave directions:
Beat egg white until foamy.
Gradually beat in half the sugar or Equal and beat until soft peaks form.
Combine tapioca, remaining sugar or Equal, milk and 1 Egg Beater in microwave bowl.
Let stand 5 minutes.
Cook at high 8-9 minutes.
Stirring every 2 minutes, until mixture comes to a full boil.
Gradually add to egg white mixture, stirring quickly just to blend.
Add vanilla.
Cool 20 minutes and serve.

Serves: 2

Nutrition per serving		Exchanges
Calories	284	1 milk
Protein	12 g.	1/2 meat
Carbohydrate	59 g.	1 starch
Cholesterol	4 mg.	1 1/2 fruit
Sodium	197 mg.	
Dietary Fiber	.1 g.	

Lori Wilson, Anaheim, California.
Operations Manager, Family Fitness Centers.

FRUIT NECTAR

ingredients: 1/2 large grapefruit
1 orange
1/2 pear
1/2 apple
1 banana

directions: Arrange on plate leaving center section open.
Put fat free cottage cheese or fat free yogurt
in center.

Serves: 2

Nutrition per serving

Calories	167
Protein	2 g.
Carbohydrate	42 g.
Cholesterol	0 mg.
Sodium	1 mg.
Dietary Fiber	6.2 g.

Exchanges
2 3/4 fruit

HOT FUDGE SUNDAE

ingredients: 1 cup fat free ice cream or yogurt
2 T. Wax Orchards fat free hot fudge sauce
1 T. Back to Nature fat free apple cinnamon granola

directions: Combine all ingredients and enjoy!

Serves: 1

Nutrition per serving

Calories	286
Protein	7 g.
Carbohydrate	63 g.
Cholesterol	0 mg.
Sodium	171 mg.
Dietary Fiber	0 g.

Exchanges
1 milk
1 starch
1 3/4 fruit

Jacie Levy, St. Louis, Missouri

FRUIT AND YOGURT

ingredients: 4 oz. Wawona frozen California blend fruit (or slices of various fresh fruits)
1 8 oz. container non fat yogurt

directions: Mix fruit with yogurt.

Variation: Add fat free granola.

Serves: 1

Nutrition per serving

Calories	215
Protein	14 g.
Carbohydrate	41 g.
Cholesterol	4 mg.
Sodium	175 mg.
Dietary Fiber	2.2 g.

Exchanges

1 milk
2 fruit

Jyl Steinback, Phoenix, Arizona

APPLE CRISP

ingredients: 4 apples, peeled and sliced
1/2 cup sugar
1 T. brown sugar
1 t. cinnamon
1/3 cup non fat dry milk
1/4 cup lemon juice
1 t. lemon extract

directions: Arrange apples in baking dish.
Sprinkle with lemon juice and extract.
Mix remaining ingredients and sprinkle over apples.
Bake for 45 minutes at 350°.

Serves: 4

Nutrition per serving

Calories	230
Protein	4 g.
Carbohydrate	55 g.
Cholesterol	2 mg.
Sodium	55 mg.
Dietary Fiber	4.1 g.

Exchanges
3 fruit
1/2 milk

FAT FREE
BANANA SPLIT

ingredients: 1 medium size banana
4 oz. of your favorite fat free ice cream or yogurt
1 T. fat free granola
1 to 2 T. Smucker's Light Hot Fudge Topping
(fat free of course)

directions: Split banana in half lengthwise and place in a bowl.
Top it with your favorite fat free ice cream or yogurt.
Add 1 to 2 T. Fat Free Smucker's Fat Free Hot Fudge
Topping.
Sprinkle fat free granola on top.

Absolutely mouth watering!

Serves: 1

Nutrition per serving		Exchanges
Calories	327	4 fruit
Protein	7 g.	1 milk
Carbohydrate	76 g.	
Cholesterol	0 mg.	
Sodium	133 mg.	
Dietary Fiber	2.7 g.	

FAT FREE
SWEET ROLL

ingredients: 1 T. Frigo fat free cheese
1 pinch cinnamon
1 pinch Sweet 'N Low
1/2 (sliced) bialy

directions: Toast bialy lightly.
On top of bialy add 1 T. Frigo.
Mix cinnamon and Sweet 'N Low together.
On top of Frigo add the mixed cinnamon
and Sweet 'N Low.

Absolutely delightful. It gets that sweet tooth
every time!

*If you can't find Frigo you may use fat free
cottage cheese.

Serves: 1

Nutrition per serving
Calories	47
Protein	6 g.
Carbohydrate	4 g.
Cholesterol	1 mg.
Sodium	16 mg.
Dietary Fiber	1.2 g.

Exchanges
1/2 starch

CARROT CAKE

ingredients:
2 cups flour
2 t. cinnamon
1 cup applesauce
1 cup Egg Beaters
3 cups coarsely grated carrots
2 cups sugar
2 t. soda
1 t. salt

directions: Sift dry ingredients, add applesauce and mix well. Add egg substitute a little at a time; beat; add carrots. Bake at 350° in well-sprayed and floured pan(s) for 35 minutes. (I find the applesauce makes this extremely moist - check at 35 minutes but may cook longer if too gooey.) Best in 2 or 3 layer cake (8 inch) pan but can be made in a 9x13x2 pan. Make a day ahead for better flavor, and refrigerate.

If desired, top with fat free cream cheese frosting:
8 oz. Fat Free Philadelphia cream cheese
16 oz. powdered sugar
2 t. vanilla
1 T. non fat or skim milk

Mix the first three ingredients and add a tablespoon of non fat milk until it is the consistency you desire. Icing is runny but yummy!

Serves: 10

Nutrition per serving (with icing)		Exchanges
Calories	425	3 1/2 fruit
Protein	8 g.	2 vegetable
Carbohydrate	99 g.	2 starch
Cholesterol	3 mg.	
Sodium	637 mg.	
Dietary Fiber	3.2 g.	

Kathy Moore, Scottsdale, Arizona

CRUSTLESS
ICE CREAM PIE

ingredients: 1/2 gallon of any flavor fat free ice cream
or yogurt
8 oz. fat free Cool Whip Lite

directions: Put ice cream into 8" or 9" pie tin and top it
with Cool Whip Lite.

Optional:
Add fat free chocolate syrup
Add bananas, strawberries, or peaches
Add fat free granola

Slice and ENJOY!

Serves: 10

Nutrition per serving
Calories	502
Protein	8 g.
Carbohydrate	51 g.
Cholesterol	7 mg.
Sodium	414 mg.
Dietary Fiber	0 g.

Exchanges
1 milk
2 1/2 starch

BLACK CHERRY ICE CREAM CAKE

ingredients: 1 Entenmann's fat free pound cake
2 cups fat free black cherry frozen yogurt
8 oz. fat free Cool Whip Lite

directions: Split cake into three layers.
Put 1/8 of a half gallon of frozen dessert
between the two layers.
Ice with Lite Cool Whip (very thin coating).
Slice and serve.

A dessert you won't want to miss!
Absolutely AWESOME!!

Nutrition per serving		Exchanges
Calories	185	1 1/4 milk
Protein	13 g.	1 starch
Carbohydrate	28 g.	
Cholesterol	7 mg.	
Sodium	359 mg.	
Dietary Fiber	0 g.	

PINEAPPLE FRUIT BOAT

ingredients:
4 cups pineapple chunks
1 cup sliced strawberries
1 cup seedless grapes
1 cup sliced banana

directions:
Hollow out both pineapples by
slicing lengthwise.
Chop pineapple in chunks.
Put in bowl and add strawberries,
grapes and bananas.
Add your favorite fat free yogurt
and blend together.
Spoon into pineapples to make your boat.
Top your Pineapple Fruit Boat with
fat free granola.

Awesome, light, and sweet as sugar!

Serves: 6

Nutrition per serving		Exchanges
Calories	109	1 3/4 fruit
Protein	1 g.	
Carbohydrate	28 g.	
Cholesterol	0 mg.	
Sodium	4 mg.	
Dietary Fiber	3.1 g.	

STUPENDOUS
STRAWBERRY FLUFF

ingredients: 2 cups strawberries

Fluff:
1/4 cup instant nonfat milk
2 t. strawberry extract
1 packet Sweet 'N Low
1/4 t. vanilla extract
1 cup crushed ice

directions: Blend in blender.
Fluff until creamy.
Add to strawberries.
Mix and serve.

Super Sensational!

Serves: 2

Nutrition per serving

Calories	102
Protein	6 g.
Carbohydrate	19 g.
Cholesterol	3 mg.
Sodium	84 mg.
Dietary Fiber	3.4 g.

Exchanges
1 3/4 fruit

CHOCOLATE MOUSSE

ingredients: 1 envelope D-Zerta Chocolate Pudding
2 envelopes Sweet 'N Low
1 T. instant coffee
1 cup non fat milk
2 T. Fat Free Smucker's Light Hot Fudge
2 T. Brandy

directions: Mix pudding, sweetener and coffee
in saucepan.
Add milk.
Stir with fork until pudding dissolves.
Add fat free hot fudge.
Place on stove, stir constantly until pudding
comes to a boil (10 minutes) and add Brandy.
Pour into serving dishes (3).

Delicious warm or cold!

Serves: 3

Nutrition per serving		Exchanges
Calories	121	1/4 milk
Protein	4 g.	1 1/4 fruit
Carbohydrate	20 g.	
Cholesterol	1 mg.	
Sodium	128 mg.	
Dietary Fiber	0 g.	

BANANA-BROWNIE SURPRISE

ingredients: 1 cup all purpose flour
1/3 cup unsweetened cocoa
1/4 cup dry milk powder non-fat
1/4 t. baking soda
1 large banana (ripe)
1 cup sugar
2 large egg whites
1/4 cup skim milk
1 t. vanilla extract

directions: Preheat oven to 350°.
Spray 9" square pan with nonstick
cooking spray.
Combine first four ingredients in bowl.
Put next five ingredients in food processor,
mix until smooth.
Add dry ingredients and mix until blended.
Pour into pan and bake 25 minutes.
Place on wire rack and cool.
Cut into 2 inch squares.

Serves: 8

Nutrition per serving		Exchanges
Calories	216	2 starch
Protein	6 g.	1 fruit
Carbohydrate	43 g.	
Cholesterol	1 mg.	
Sodium	78 mg.	
Dietary Fiber	.3 g.	

PUMPKIN PUDDING

ingredients: 1/2 cup canned pumpkin
1 cup fat free vanilla yogurt
1/4 t. ground cinnamon

directions: Mix all ingredients until well blended.
Garnish with cinnamon sticks. (optional)

Serves: 1

Nutrition per serving
Calories	249
Protein	13 g.
Carbohydrate	50 g.
Cholesterol	4 mg.
Sodium	162 mg.
Dietary Fiber	3.7 g.

Exchanges
1 milk
2 vegetable

PEACH MOLD

ingredients:
1 1/2 cups boiling water
2 packages peach Jell-o (4 serving size)
2 cups ice cubes
2 cups halved peaches
1 cup Cool Whip Lite

directions:
Pour boiling water into blender.
Add Jell-o.
Blend at low speed until dissolved.
Add ice cubes.
Stir until almost dissolved.
Add peaches and Cool Whip Light.
Blend at High speed until smooth.
Pour into Jell-o mold and chill until set.
Unmold and garnish with peaches.

Recipe can be doubled for larger mold.

Serves: 4

Nutrition per serving

Calories	92
Protein	1 g.
Carbohydrate	18 g.
Cholesterol	0 mg.
Sodium	32 mg.
Dietary Fiber	1.2 g.

Exchanges
1 1/2 fruit

STRAWBERRY PARFAIT

ingredients: 3/4 cup Fat Free cottage cheese
2 t. sugar
1/2 t. almond extract
1/4 t. ground cinnamon
1 cup sliced fresh strawberries
2 T. fat free granola
2 T. fresh strawberries

directions: Combine first 4 ingredients in a blender.
Blend until smooth.
Place 1/4 cup strawberries into parfait glass.
Top with 3 T. cheese mixture
Repeat, then top with 1 T. granola

Makes 2 servings.
Garnish each with a strawberry.

Nutrition per serving		Exchanges
Calories	101	1 fruit
Protein	11 g.	1 meat
Carbohydrate	15 g.	
Cholesterol	4 mg.	
Sodium	264 mg.	
Dietary Fiber	2.1 g.	

CHERRY COMPOTE

ingredients: 1 T. cornstarch
1/4 cup cold water
2 T. sugar
2 t. lemon juice
2 cups fresh or frozen strawberries (whole)
3 cups pitted dark cherries halved
or 1 pound package frozen pitted dark cherries

directions: Sauce:
Cook and stir (in medium saucepan) cornstarch
and water until thick, about 2 minutes.
Remove from heat.
Add sugar, lemon juice, almond extract and stir.
Halve large strawberries.
Add to sauce with cherries and stir.
Put in bowl, cover and chill 2 to 24 hours.

Serves: 4

Nutrition per serving		**Exchanges**
Calories	160	2 1/2 fruit
Protein	2 g.	
Carbohydrate	40 g.	
Cholesterol	0 mg.	
Sodium	3 mg.	
Dietary Fiber	3 g.	

FRUIT BAVARIAN

ingredients: 1 (3 oz. package) strawberry gelatin
2 cups fat free frozen strawberry yogurt
1/4 cup brandy

directions: Dissolve gelatin in 1 cup boiling water.
Add frozen yogurt in large spoonfuls and
stir until melted.
Add Brandy.
Pour into 4 serving dishes and chill until set.

Serves: 4

Nutrition per serving

Calories	205
Protein	5 g.
Carbohydrate	38 g.
Cholesterol	0 mg.
Sodium	104 mg.
Dietary Fiber	0 g.

Exchanges
2 1/2 fruit
1/2 milk

DESIRABLE
DRINKS

BANANA SHAKE

ingredients: 2 ripe bananas
1/2 cup skim milk
1 t. Sweet 'N Low (optional)
1 T. fat free chocolate syrup
8-10 ice cubes

directions: Combine banana, skim milk, Sweet 'N Low, and chocolate syrup in blender.
Cover and mix for 1 minute.
Add ice cubes, one at a time, mixing until smooth.

Serves: 2

Nutrition per serving

Calories	155
Protein	4 g.
Carbohydrate	37 g.
Cholesterol	1 mg.
Sodium	54 mg.
Dietary Fiber	2.7 g.

Exchanges
2 fruit
1/4 milk

RASPBERRY
ICED TEA

ingredients: 1-10 oz.bag frozen raspberries
6 tea bags
3 cinnamon sticks
1 orange, sliced
3 1/2 quarts water

directions: Boil water.
Place tea bags in boiling water.
Remove tea bags.
Add all remaining ingredients.
Add Equal to taste.

Serves: 6

Nutrition per serving
Calories	70
Protein	1 g.
Carbohydrate	19 g.
Cholesterol	0 mg.
Sodium	5 mg.
Dietary Fiber	5.2 g.

Exchanges
1 fruit

Karen Snedeker, Minneapolis, Minnesota. "I have been an aerobic instructor for eight years. I am the service manager at Bally's U.S. Fitness."

ORANGE DELIGHT

ingredients: 1 cup orange juice
1/3 cup instant non fat dry milk
3 or 4 ice cubes
1/4 t. vanilla

directions: Put all ingredients in blender and mix on high for
15 to 30 seconds or until ice is crushed.

Optional: Leave out ice and add frozen fruit, like
strawberries, bananas, blueberries, or raspberries for
a thick milk shake consistency (1/2 cup per serving).

Optional: Add 1/2 cup drained pineapple and 1/4 t.
coconut extract for piña colada flavor.

Serves: 1

Nutrition per serving

Calories	188
Protein	8.9 g.
Carbohydrate	36.8 g.
Cholesterol	3.6 mg.
Sodium	114 mg.
Dietary Fiber	1.9 g.

Exchanges
2 1/3 fruit
1/3 milk

*Linda Smith, aerobics and fitness walking instructor,
host of the "Walking Program" on KGNX radio,
OK IDEA state representative, wife and mother of
2 beautiful young girls.*

HOT HOLIDAY PUNCH

---

ingredients: 1 1/2 cups apples juice
1 1/2 cups orange juice
3 cupa cranberry juice cocktail
3/4 cup maple syrup
2 t. powdered sugar
1 1/2 t. ground cinnamon
3/4 t. ground cloves
3/4 t. ground nutmet

directions: Combine all ingredients in a heavy saucepan and bring to a boil.
Reduce heat to low and simmer 10-15 minutes.

Serves: 10

Nutrition per serving		**Exchanges**
Calories	144	2 1/2 fruit
Protein	.3 g.	
Carbohydrate	36 g.	
Cholesterol	0 mg.	
Sodium	6 mg.	
Dietary Fiber	.5 g.	

HAWAIIAN SMOOTHIE

ingredients: 1 papaya
                    1 banana
                    1/2 cup plain fat free yogurt
                    1/2 cup apple juice
                    crushed ice

directions: Blend all ingredients in a blender.
                    Enjoy!

                    Serves: 2

Nutrition per serving

Calories	173
Protein	5 g.
Carbohydrate	40 g.
Cholesterol	1 mg.
Sodium	50 mg.
Dietary Fiber	4.2 g.

Exchanges

2 fruit
1/2 milk

Rebecca Lunden-Draeger, Kailua, Hawaii.
RLD Body Works,

173

PATIO FREEZE

ingredients:
1 cup sugar
1 can crushed pineapple and juice
2 cups orange juice
2 cups mashed bananas
2 T. lemon juice
10-12 chopped maraschino cherries

directions:
Mix all together in freezer bowl.
When frozen almost solid, work with a spoon
and refreeze.

Variation: Pour diet 7-up over a cup of Patio Freeze.

Serves: 8

Nutrition per serving		**Exchanges**
Calories	242	4 fruit
Protein	1 g.	
Carbohydrate	62 g.	
Cholesterol	0 mg.	
Sodium	17 mg.	
Dietary Fiber	2.1 g.	

*Sherrie Veach, exercise physiologist working in cardiac
rehab at Scottsdale Memorial Hospital and fitness
instructor at Paradise Valley Community College.*

STRAWBERRY SHAKE

ingredients: 10 oz. frozen unsweetened strawberries
1/2 cup skim milk
1/4 cup vanilla flavored non fat yogurt
1 t. sugar or sweetener to taste

directions: Blend all ingredients at high speed in blender until smooth.

Absolutely SMASHING!!

Serves: 2

Nutrition per serving		Exchanges
Calories	166	2 fruit
Protein	4 g.	1/2 milk
Carbohydrate	40 g.	
Cholesterol	2 mg.	
Sodium	52 mg.	
Dietary Fiber	2.7 g.	

MAGNIFICENT MENU

DAY 1 - MONDAY

BREAKFAST
    1 piece "Unfrench" Toast - page 51
    1/2 cup fat free cottage cheese
    1 piece of your favorite fruit

MID-MORNING SNACK
    1 Bialy bagel
    2 slices of fat free cheese

LUNCH
    broccoli soup - page 137
    fat free crackers
    raspberry ice tea

MID-AFTERNOON SNACK
    vegetables cut up (carrots, celery, cauliflower,
    and broccoli)
    cottage cheese dip - page 6

DINNER
    4 oz. of your favorite fish (marinated) - page 103
    tomato salad
    Spanish rice - page 72
    1 slice toasted sourdough bread

DESSERT
    1 cup frozen grapes

What a wonderful day you had.
FAT FREE AND FABULOUS!!
I am proud of you. Keep up the great job!

DAY 2 - TUESDAY

BREAKFAST
   Veggie Egg Beater omelet - page 54
   1 toasted Bialy (with Butter Buds)
   1 cup fruit juice

MID-MORNING SNACK
   1 cup yogurt with slices of banana

LUNCH
   Caesar salad - page 23 or page 39
   fat free croutons (a healthy hand full) - page 24
   crunchy blueberry muffin - page 88

MID-AFTERNOON SNACK
   air popcorn - page 130

DINNER
   pasta with red pepper lentil sauce - page 104
   garlic cheese bread - page 87
   steamed artichoke - page 63

DESSERT
   fat free fabulous yogurt

I think you are Absolutely AWESOME!

DAY 3 - WEDNESDAY

BREAKFAST
  mushroom Egg Beater Omelet
  1 spicy muffin - page 93
  1 glass of fresh juice

MID-MORNING SNACK
  1 apple

LUNCH
  mushroom barley soup - page 140

MID-AFTERNOON SNACK
  skinny dip with cut up vegetables

DINNER
  4 oz. of your favorite fish
  Spanish rice - page 72
  green bean surprise - page 67
  small marinated salad - page 25

DESSERT
  ice cream cake - page 144

What an exciting day you had! You really are outdoing yourself!
GOOD FOR YOU!

DAY 4 - THURSDAY

BREAKFAST
    fried matzo with 1 piece of fat free Swiss cheese -
    page 53
    5 apricots

MID-MORNING SNACK
    banana shake with non fat spice muffin - page
    169 & page 93

LUNCH
    rice teriyaki - page 74
    stir-fried vegetables

MID-AFTERNOON SNACK
    1 fat free yogurt

DINNER
    quick and easy pasta dish - page 108
    mexi cornbread - page 89
    spinach salad with mandarin dressing - page 32
    and fat free croutons - page 24

DESSERT
    apple coffee cake - page 148

You are a super special somebody! Give yourself a big HUG!

DAY 5 - FRIDAY

BREAKFAST
    cold cereal (under 1 gram of fat)
    1 cup skim milk or non fat milk
    bran muffin - page 90 or page 98
    1/2 banana (add to cold cereal if desire)

MID-MORNING SNACK
    1 bialy bagel with fat free cream cheese

LUNCH
    vegetable quiche - page 110
    minestrone soup by Pritkins

MID-AFTERNOON SNACK
    1 bowl of fabulous fruit in season
    1/2 cup cottage cheese
    (my favorite is 1/2 cantaloupe scooped out with
    the cottage cheese in the center)

DINNER
    garlic scallops and angel hair pasta - page 111
    sourdough garlic bread
    spinach stuffed mushrooms - page 21

DESSERT
    Snackwells devil's food cookie
    glass of skim or non fat milk

What a FUN day you had! Don't you feel GREAT ABOUT YOURSELF!

DAY 6 - SATURDAY

BREAKFAST
    Cream of Wheat
    small box of raisins
    cinnamon to season
    1 glass skim or non fat milk

MID-MORNING SNACK
    vegetables (carrots, celery cauliflower,
    broccoli, etc.)
    spinach dip

LUNCH
    pita pizza - page 116
    gazpacho soup - page 142

MID-AFTERNOON SNACK
    fat free chips - page 1
    salsa dip - page 3

DINNER
    shrimp scramble - page 115
    sliced potatoes - page 75
    squash salad - page 36

DESSERT
    frozen banana

Your fat free eating is becoming a HABIT and you really are doing OUTSTANDING! Super job!

DAY 7 - SUNDAY

BREAKFAST
> stir-fried veggie omelet - page 56
> 1 bialy bagel toasted with jelly
> a glass orange juice

MID-MORNING SNACK
> fat free yogurt with fat free granola

LUNCH
> pocket bread sandwich
> Healthy Valley 14 Garden Vegetable
> fat free croutons to put in soup - page 24

MID-AFTERNOON SNACK
> fruit kabob and dip - page 133

DINNER
> pasta stir fry - page 106
> dinner salad

DESSERT
> banana brownie sundae - page 147

You made it a whole week! Aren't you the GREATEST!
CONGRATULATIONS! KEEP UP THE GOOD JOB!

FABULOUS
FAT COUNTER

SOME OF
MY FAVORITE
FAT FREE FOODS

1. Fat Free Fig Newtons by Nabisco Foods (also Apple Newtons)
2. Snack Wells: Cinnamon Graham Snacks, Wheat Crackers, and Devil's Food Cookie Cakes.
3. Betty Crocker Chiffon Lemon Cake Mix, Confetti Angel Food Cake Mix, and White Angel Food Cake
4. Fat Free Light Life Meatless Smart Dogs
5. Pretzenality - Snyder's Hard Pretzels of Hanover
6. Kangaroo Sandwich Pocket Bread (whole wheat or white), located in Deli-Bakery section
7. Butter Buds
8. Best of Butter (Natural Cheddar Cheese or Sour Cream)
9. Fat Free Quaker Butter Popped Corn Cakes (also Caramel and White Cheddar)
10. Smucker's Light Hot Fudge Topping
11. Fat Free Granola (packages or bulk)
12. Fat Free Saltine Crackers
13. Deluxe Vegetarian Beans
14. Dairy:
    a. Knudson Fat Free Cottage Cheese
    b. Knudson Fat Free Sour Cream
    c. Fat Free Yogurt
        A. La Corona
        B. Dannon
        C. Yoplait
    d. Fat Free Philadelphia Cream Cheese
    e. Alpine Lace Free n' Lean Cheeses
    f. Fat Free Kraft Slices
    g. Fat Free Borden slices: Swiss and sharp cheddar
    h. Fat Free Smart Beat: American flavor
    i. Healthy Choice Fat Free, individually wrapped singles or pound processed cheese
    j. Healthy Choice, Fat Free Cream Cheese (box or soft)
    k. Healthy Choice, Fat Free Shredded or String Cheese
    l. Weight Watchers Fat Free Parmesan Cheese
15. Frozen Section:
    a. Super Pretzel
    b. Dryers Fat Free Vanilla
    c. Dryers Non Fat Frozen Yogurt Inspiration
    d. Kemps Frozen Yogurt

SOME OF
MY FAVORITE
FAT FREE FOODS

e. Frozen Yogurt Non Fat Mix
f. Fruit and Yogurt Frozfruit (Pineapple and Strawberry)
g. Premium Classic Fat Free Frozen Dessert
h. Fat Free Kellogg's Waffles from Eggo
i. Yoplait Vanilla Orange Cremes Frozen Dairy Dessert (and chocolate mousse flavor)
j. Simple Pleasures Light Frozen Dairy Dessert (variety of flavors)
k. Smucker's Fruitage Frozen Dessert (boysenberry, peach)
l. Dole Sorbet Fruit Ice (raspberry, strawberry flavors)
m. Weight Watchers Fat Free Ice cream

16. Entenmann's - all fat free desserts
17. Hain Fat Free Soup (Mushroom Barley)
18. Pritikins: Tomato and Minestrone Soups
19. Weight Watcher's Spaghetti Sauce with Mushrooms
20. Healthy Valley products: soups, crackers, cereal, corn puffs, etc.
21. Smucker's Frozen Dessert Fruitage
22. Hershey's Fat Free Chocolate Bar Flavor Puddings
23. Fat Free Jell-o
24. Bialy Bagel
25. No Fat Granola Back to Nature (apple cinnamon or natural)
26. Childers Natural Potato Chips 100% fat free
27. Frigo Truly Lite Fat Free Ricotta
28. Weight Watcher's Instant Nonfat Dry Milk Dairy Creamer
29. Fat Free Swiss Miss hot cocoa mix
30. 10 Bran Cereal by Health Valley Fat Free (apple, regular or almond)
31. Health Valley Fat-Free Granola Bars (6 delicious flavors)
32. Guiltless Gourmet Picante Sauce (mild, medium or hot)
33. Health Valley Fat Free Cookies (6 flavors)
34. Nabisco Mr. Phipps Fat Free Pretzel Chips
35. Fat Free Pasta Sauce by Tree of Life
36. Fat Free Cheese Puffs by Healthy Valley (3 flavors)
37. Fat Free RW Frookie Gourmet Water Cracker (garlic & herb and cracked pepper)
38. Fat Free Frookie Cookies (apples spice, oatmeal raisin, and cranberry orange)
39. Promise Fat Free Butter
40. Wonder Light White Fat Free Bread

SOME OF
MY FAVORITE
FAT FREE FOODS

41. Weight Watcher's Fat Free Mayonnaise
42. Louise's Fat Free Caramel Corn
43. Louise's Mesquite Barbecue Potato Chips
44. Burns & Ricker Fat Free Party Mix
45. Burns & Ricker Fat Free Garlic Bagel Chips
46. Hershey's Fat Free Pudding
47. Land O' Lakes No Fat Sour Cream
48. Smart Temptations Fat Free Lemon Pepper Salad Dressing
49. Marzetti's Fat Free Honey Dijon Salad Dressing
50. Oscar Mayer Healthy Favorites Smoked Turkey Breast
51. Fat Free Louis Rich Smoked Hickory Turkey
52. Hillshire Farms Fat Free Smoked Chicken Breast
53. Healthy Favorites Kraft Fat Free Shredded Cheddar Cheese
54. Kellogg's Corn Flake Crumbs
55. Louis Kemp Fat Free Seafood Crab Delight
56. Louis Kemp Fat Free Lobster Delight
57. Nabisco Cracker Meal
58. Success Rice 10 Minute Natural Long Grain
59. Townhouse Instant Rice
60. Heinz Fat Free Gravy (Chicken, Turkey or Beef)
61. Fat Free Pasta Sauce by Tree of Life
62. Fat Free Father Sam's Pocket Bread
63. Fat Free Buena Vida Flour Tortillas
64. Fat Free T Marzettis Poppyseed Salad Dressing
65. Fat Free T Marzettis Caesar Salad Dressing
66. Krusteaz Fat Free Wild Berry and Apple Cinnamon Muffins
67. Betty Crocker Wild Blueberry Fat Free Muffins
68. Angel Food Cake Mix
69. Pioneer Biscuit and Baking Mix
70. Pioneer No-Fat Country Gravy Mix
71. No-Fat Brown Gravy Mix
72. Fat Free Sliced Red Potato Salad by Reser's Fine Foods found in Deli Departments in your supermarket
73. Fat Free Black Bean Salsa Salad by Reser's Fine Foods found in Deli Departments in your supermarket
74. Fat Free Country Potato Salad by Reser's Fine Foods found in Deli Departments in your supermarket
75. Fat Free Pasta Prima Vera Salad by Reser's Fine Foods found in Deli Departments in your supermarket
76. Fat Free Original and Butter Toffee Cracker Jacks

SOME OF
MY FAVORITE
FAT FREE FOODS

77. Fat Free Fleischmann's
78. Heinz Fat Free Chicken Gravy
79. No-Fat Dips (ranch, salsa and French onion by Land-O-Lakes
80. Fat Free B & M Baked Beans
81. Fat Free Hershey's Chocolate Shoppe Sundae Syrup
82. Fat Free Coffee-Mate (non-dairy creamer) by Carnation
83. Oscar Mayer Fat Free Bologna

A HEALTHY EATING PLAN WITH NO FATS

FISH

High in Protein, B Vitamins and Iron and other Minerals

	ounces	total fats
Abalone, canned	3 1/2 oz.	0.3
Clams,		
canned, solids and liquid	1/2 cup	0.7
meat only	5 large	0.9
Cod		
canned	3 1/2 oz.	0.3
cooked	3 1/2 oz.	0.3
Crab		
Crappie, white	3 1/2 oz.	0.8
Crayfish		
freshwater	3 1/2 oz.	0.5
Cusk		
steamed	3 1/2 oz.	0.7
Dolphin Fish	3 1/2 oz.	0.7
Flatfish	3 1/2 oz.	0.8
Flounder		
Sole	3 1/2 oz.	0.5
Haddock		
cooked	3 1/2 oz.	0.6
smoked/canned	3 1/2 oz.	0.4
Octopus	3 1/2 oz.	0.8
Perch, freshwater		
yellow	3 1/2 oz.	0.9
Pickerel	3 1/2 oz.	0.5
Pike		
Blue	3 1/2 oz.	0.9
Shrimp		
canned, wet pack	1/2 cup	0.8
Sole, fillet	3 1/2 oz.	0.5

EGGS
High in Protein, B Vitamins and Iron

Substitute, frozen Egg Beaters	1/4 cup	0.0
Egg white	1 large	0.0

VEGETABLES AND FRUITS
High in Vitamins, Minerals and Fiber
Low in fat, calories and Sodium ... contain no cholesterol

All fruits are under 1 gram of fat except for avocados (using serving size of 1/2 to 1 cup).

All vegetables, raw, cooked or steamed, are under 1 gram of fat except for avocados (using 1/2 to 1 cup).

MILK PRODUCTS
High in Protein, Calcium, Phosphorus, Niacin, Riboflavin, Vitamins A and D

Buttermilk Dry (only)	1 T.	0.4
Evaporated Milk		
skim	1/2 cup	0.4
Hot Cocoa		
low cal, mix with water	1 cup	0.8
Skim Milk		
liquid	1 cup	0.4
nonfat dry powder	1/4 cup	0.2
Yogurt:		
La Corona Fat Free	1 cup	0.0
Dannon Lowfat and Fat Free	1 cup	0.0
Yoplait Fat Free	1 cup	0.0
Frozen Non Fat	1/2 cup	0.2
Fruits and Yogurt Frozfruit	1 bar	0.0
Dryers Fat Free	4 oz.	0.0

Dryers Non Fat Frozen		
Yogurt Inspiration	4 oz.	0.0
Kemps Frozen Yogurt No Fat	4 oz.	0.0
Frozen Yogurt Non Fat Mix		
Premium Classic Fat Free		
Frozen Dessert	4 oz.	0.0
Cheeses:		
Alpine Lace, Free n' Lean		
Mozzarella	1 oz.	0.0
American	1 oz.	0.0
Cheddar	1 oz.	0.0
Parmesan	1 oz.	0.0
Borden		
Swiss	1 oz.	0.0
Sharp Cheddar	1 oz.	0.0
Kraft Fat Free Singles	1 oz.	0.0
Cottage Cheese		
Knudsen Fat Free	4 oz.	0.0
Sour Cream		
Knudsen Fat Free	1 oz.	0.0

BREADS, CEREALS, PASTA AND STARCHY VEGETABLES
Low in fat and cholesterol; High in B Vitamins, Iron and Fiber

Boston Brown Bread	1/2 in. slice	0.6
Breadsticks	1 piece	0.2
plain	1 piece	0.2
soft type	1 medium	0.1
Bread		
Italian	1 slice	0.5
Lite Varieties	1 slice	0.
Mixed grain	1 slice	0
Pita, plain	1 large	
Rye, American	1 slice	
Rye, Pumpernickel	1 slice	
Sourdough	1 slice	

Crackers

matzos	1 board	0.9
melba toast	1 piece	0.2
Norwegian flatbread	2 thin	0.3
Premium fat free crackers	5 crackers	0.0
rice cakes	1 piece	0.3
rice wafer	3 wafers	0.0
Ryekrisp, plain	2 crackers	0.2
Saltines	2 crackers	0.6
Snack Wells Wheat Crackers fat free		
zwieback	2 crackers	0.7

Rolls:

French	1 small	0.4

Tortilla:

Corn (baked)	1 medium	0.8

Cereals:

Apple Jacks	1 cup	0.1
Bran Buds	1/3 cup	0.7
Bran Flakes 40%	1 cup	0.1
Bran, unprocessed, dry	1/4 cup	0.6
Corn Chex	1 cup	0.1
Corn Flakes	1 cup	0.1
Corn Grits	1/2 cup	0.5
Cream of Wheat	1/2 cup	0.3
Fruit Loops	1 cup	0.0
Frosted Mini-Wheats	4 biscuits	0.3
Fruit & Fibre	1/2 cup	0.3
Grapenut Flakes	1 cup	0.2
Grapenuts	3/4 cup	0.7
Honeynut Cheerios	3/4 cup	0.7
Kix	1 1/2 cups	0.7
Nutri-Grain	3/4 cups	0.2 - 0.7
Puffed Rice	1 cup	0.0
Puffed Wheat	1 cup	0.1
Raisin Bran	1 cup	0.8
Rice Chex	1 cup	0.1

Rice Krispies	1 cup	0.5
Shredded Wheat	1 cup	0.5
Shredded Wheat Squares	1/2 cup	0.0
Special K	1 cup	0.1
Sugar Frosted Flakes	1 cup	0.0
Sugar Smacks	3/4 cups	0.5
Team	1 cup	0.5
Total	1 cup	0.7
Wheaties	1 cup	0.5
Soups:		
Beef Broth	1 cup	0.5
Consomme with Gelatin	1 cup	0.0
Dehydrated:		
Beef Noodle	1 cup	0.8
Boullion Cube, Beef	1 cube	0.3
Boullion Cube, Chicken	1 cube	0.2
Onion, Prepared	1 cup	0.6
Pea, Split	1 cup	0.6
Hain Soups Fat Free		0.0
Healthy Valley Fat Free Soups		0.0
Snacks:		
Popcorn (air-popped)	1 cup	0.0
Fig Newton Fat Free by Nabisco		
Regular and Apple		0.0
Pretzenality, Snyder's of Hanover Hard Pretzels		0.0

FATS AND OILS

Some of these foods are high in vitamins A or E, but all are high in fat and calories.

Butter Buds	2 T.	0.0
Best O' Butter	1/2 T.	0.9
cheddar cheese		
sour cream		
Mazola No Stick Spray	2 1/2 secs.	0.9
Cream Substitute, Powdered	1 T.	0.7

DESSERTS

Fruits		
Entenmann's Fat Free Desserts	1 oz. slice	0.0
Angel Food	1/12 cake	0.2
Cookies:		
Arrowroot	1	0.9
Rice Krispie Bar	1	0.9
SnackWells		
Cinnamon Graham Snacks		
Devil's Food Cookie Cakes		
Betty Crocker Chiffon Lemon Cake Mix		0.0
Confetti Angel Food Cake Mix		0.0
White Angel Food Cake		0.0
Premium Classic Fat Free Frozen Dessert		0.0
Dryers Fat Free Ice Cream		0.0
Dryers NonFat Frozen Yogurt Inspiration		0.0
Kemps - Frozen Yogurt No Fat		0.0
Frozen Yogurt Non Fat Mix		0.0
Fruits and Yogurt Frozfruit No Fat		0.0
Popcorn Cakes - Quaker Fat Free		
Caramel or Butter Popped Corn		0.0
Fruit Ice, Italian	1/2 cup	0.0
Fudgesicles, no fat		0.0
Gelatin	1/2 cup	0.0
Fat Free Granola		0.0
Popsicle	1 bar	0.0
Pudding:		
From mix with skim milk	1.2 cp	0.0
Toppings:		
Butterscotch/caramel	3 T.	0.1
Cherry	3 T.	0.1
Chocolate Syrup Hershey	2 T.	0.4
Marshmallow Creme	3 T.	0.0
Hard Candies		0.0

Sources gathered from: The American Heart Association Diet, 7272 Greenville Avenue, Dallas, Texas 72531-4596 and the T-Factor Fat Gram Counter by Jamie Pope-Cordle and Martin Katahn, W.V. Norton and Company, New York.

Index